# Sex Pistols

## Retrospective

RETRO PUBLISHING

Published by:

RETRO PUBLISHING
P.O. Box 5
16 Notting Hill Gate
London W11 3JE

All rights reserved. No part of this book may be reproduced in any form or by any Electronic or mechanical means, including information storage or retrieval systems, without prior permission in writing from the publisher, except by a reviewer who may quote brief passages.

# CONTENTS

| | |
|---|---|
| Introduction | 5 |
| A Brief History | 7 |
| Anarchy in the UK | 13 |
| God Save the Queen | 18 |
| Pretty Vacant | 25 |
| Holidays in the Sun | 31 |
| Submission/New York | 33 |
| Lentilmas Flexi | 33 |
| No One is Innocent/The Biggest Blow/My Way | 34 |
| Something Else/Friggin' in the Riggin' | 37 |
| Silly Thing | 38 |
| You Need Hands | 40 |
| Heritage EP | 40 |
| C'mon Everybody | 41 |
| The Great Rock'n'Roll Swindle | 42 |
| (I'm not your) Stepping Stone | 43 |
| Sex Pistols 6-Pack | 44 |
| The Heyday Cassette | 46 |
| Who Killed Bambi | 46 |
| Sub-mission/No Feelings | 47 |
| Sub-mission/Anarchy in the UK | 48 |
| Never Mind the Bollocks - The Full Story | 49 |
| The Great Rock'n'Roll Swindle - The Whole Story | 61 |
| Some Product - Carri on Sex Pistols | 71 |
| The Very Best of Sex Pistols | 72 |
| Flogging a Dead Horse | 73 |
| The Mini Album | 74 |
| The Original Sex Pistols Live | 76 |
| Better Live Than Dead | 77 |
| The Swindle Continues | 78 |
| Party Till you Puke | 79 |
| Live at Chelmsford Prison | 80 |
| Kiss This | 81 |
| Sex Pistols Bootleg Bible | 82 |
| Sid Vicious Alive and Well | 90 |
| Sex Pistols Gig Guide ... Confirmed Sightings | 91 |
| "Never Mind the Sex Pistols ... Here's the Filthy Lucre" | 95 |

anarchy in the USA

nashville         100 club

screen on the green

jubilee boat trip

el paradise

paradise club

never mind the bans

lafayette club

spots tour

st martins school of art

lesser free trade hall

eric's         ivanhoe's club

chelmsford prison

# Introduction

The dust has settled, it's time to take stock to deal with the past. The Sex Pistols came, saw and exploded onto the scene, became public enemy Number 1, rode the crest of the wave and disappeared in true chaotic fashion.

It's hard to believe that TVs were kicked in and strikes caused all in their name. They were the last Rock'n'Roll band that signified change. Never before or since has music, style, art, youth and social statement peaked at the same time.

Cynics say nothing's changed since their arrival and departure. But as most innovators of today's music/media scene will confirm, it was either through seeing or being inspired by the Pistols that motivated their initial moves.

The Sex Pistols were very much a vinyl orientated phenomenon. So sit back and enjoy flicking through these pages and be amused at how many different releases around the world a band can muster through, basically two album releases. It's taken twenty years to collate this information and track down many of these deleted releases due to the group's upheavals and label changes. Putting on the editor's hat for a moment just to say, what was left on the editing floor was due to being (a) 2nd/3rd reissue rubbish (Hello Jock) or (b) like the Holy Grail still not been unearthed.

Like history itself, the story continues. All we need now is a reformation tour, a double live album and we're off again. Don't look over your shoulder ... here comes the filthy lucre.

So when somebody asks you in years to come what was a Sex Pistol, while showing them the numerous excellent books on the subject, `England's dreaming' by Jon Savage for one, please dust down this volume and let them browse through it and say for the long and short of it, this is what the lads got up to.

    Enjoy,

# your friendly

# agent provocateur.

# manifesto

Lesson 1 — how to manufacture your group

Lesson 2 — establish the name

Lesson 3 — how to sell the swindle

Lesson 4 — do not play do not give the game away

Lesson 5 — get off the label as quick as possible get as much money as you can

Lesson 6 — how to become the greatest tourist attraction

Lesson 7 — cultivate hatred

Lesson 8 — how to diversify your business... what a business

Lesson 9 — take civilization to the barbarians

Lesson 10 — who killed bambi

# A Brief History

## Summer 1975

The 'Swankers' are formed. Helped through meetings in 'sex' boutique run by Malcolm McLaren and Vivienne Westwood.

Line up      Glen Matlock (bass) Sex Shop Saturday boy
                Steven Jones (vocals)
                Paul Cook (drums)
                Wally Nightingale (guitar)

Only public gig - 3 songs at a party above Tom Salter's cafe on Kings Road, Chelsea.

## August 1975

A recent regular customer with green hair and attitude, John Lydon, is asked to audition in a nearby pub, The Roebuck. He sings along to Alice Cooper's 'Eighteen' in front of the Juke Box. He's in ...

New Name    Sex Pistols
New line up   Glen Matlock (bass)
                 Steve Jones (guitar)
                 Paul Cook (drums)
                 Johnny Rotten (vocals)

## 6 November 1975

Group debut gig, St Martin's School of Art in London.

## 12 February 1976

Sex Pistols support Eddie and the Hot Rods at the Marquee Club.

## 14 February 1976

Play the famous Andrew Logan's party.

## 30 March 1976

Sex Pistols debut 100 Club.

## 3 April 1976

Debut Nashville Rooms supporting Joe Strummers, then Group 101'ers

## 4 June 1976

Play Manchester, Lesser Free Trade Hall.

## 13-30 July 1976

Record demos with Dave Goodman in Denmark Street (see mini LP release).

# A Brief History

### 20 July 1976

Play Lesser Free Trade Hall. First time `Anarchy in the UK' is aired in public.

### 29 August 1976

Sex Pistols stage a concert with the Clash (their first London gig) and the Buzzcocks at the Screen on the Green in Islington.

### 3 September 1976

First foreign gig, The Club de Chalet de Lac, Paris, France.

### 4 September 1976

Sex Pistols TV debut on `So it goes' singing `Anarchy in the UK'.

### 17 September 1976

Sex Pistols play at Chelmsford Maximum Security Prison.

### 20 September 1976

Sex Pistols headline the 100 Club Punk Festival, first night with the Clash and Suzi & The Banshees featuring Sid Vicious on drums.

### 24 September 1976

Play Burton-upon-Trent 76 Club. The legendary `Indecent Exposure' bootleg later to be officially released as `The Original Pistols Live'.

### 8 October 1976

Sex Pistols sign to EMI for £40,000.

### 17 October 1976

Sex Pistols record `Anarchy in the UK' in Wessex Studios with producer Chris Thomas.

### 26 November 1976

`Anarchy in the UK/I wanna be me' released. It will rise to Number 38 before being deleted.

### 1 December 1976

Sex Pistols appear on `Today' programme. The legendary Grundy interview takes place. `Punk goes Public'.

### 3 December 1976

`Anarchy in the UK' tour is scheduled to start. Due to the uproar over the TV show, only three of the 19 planned shows will be played.

# A Brief History

**4 January 1977**

Sex Pistols cause rumpus at Heathrow Airport on their way to Amsterdam to play three concerts and do TV work.

**6 January 1977**

EMI terminate Sex Pistols' contract.

**7 January 1977**

Sex Pistols play Paradiso Club Amsterdam
History tells us this is to be Glen Matlock's last gig as a Sex Pistol.

**4 February 1977**

It's official Glen Matlock is out. Sid Vicious is in.

**9 March 1977**

Sex Pistols sign to A&M Records for £150,000 outside Buckingham Palace.

**16 March 1977**

A&M terminate Sex Pistols' contract. Band get £25,000 compensation and the £50,000 advance = £75,000. Not bad for a week's work.
Malcolm's classic quote "I keep walking in and out of offices being given cheques".

**25 March 1977**

The date `God Save the Queen' on A&M would have been released but alas all got destroyed ... or did they???

**13 May 1977**

Sex Pistols sign to Richard Branson's Hippy label, Virgin Records. Sid signs on the 16th, as he's ill in hospital.

**27 May 1977**

Virgin release `God save the Queen'.

**8 June 1977**

Infamous Sex Pistols Boat Party. Band play `Anarchy in the UK' when their boat reaches the Houses of Parliament.

**17 June 1977**

`God save the Queen/Did you no wrong' reaches Number 2 in the Charts. Rumour has it that it's sold more records than Rod Stewart, but is held off the Number 1 spot.

# A Brief History

### 2 July 1977

`Pretty Vacant/No Fun' is released. It will climb to Number 6 in the Charts.

### 15 October 1977

`Holidays in the Sun/Satellite' is released. It will reach Number 8 in the Charts.

### 20 October 1977

Holidays sleeve is withdrawn due to copyright problems with a Belgium travel company.

### 28 October 1977

`Never mind the Bollocks' is released and instantly qualifies for a Gold Disc. Over 100,000 sales. Not bad considering advertisements are banned and displaying the LP causing so many problems. Enters UK Charts at Number 1 displacing Cliff Richard's 40 Golden Greats.
Talk of two versions of the album due to ban from the major chains - Woolworths, Boots and W.H. Smith (see N.M.T.B. Chapter for both these stories).

### 30 October 1977

Ideas for a film about the group initially called `Who Killed Bambi' get set back when Russ Meyer (yes, him), American porn producer, gives up the idea, to many clashes with Malcolm and Rotten and flies home to USA.

### November 1977

Pistols sign American record deal with Warner Bros, USA. After a brief trip to Europe for gigs the Pistols' return to play some gigs in England under the banner `Never mind the Bans', this will culminate with a gig at Ivanhoes Club in Huddersfield on 25 December, Xmas Day. This will turn out to be the Sex Pistols' last UK gig.

### January 1978

`Never mind the Bollocks' rises the US Charts to Number 106.

### 3 January 1978

After initial visor problems (ie. they all have `records'), they get the O.K. and head to the USA to conquer the world.

### 14 January 1978

Just seven gigs later (see `Gig Guide' chapter for more details), Sex Pistols will play their last ever gig at Winterland Ballroom, Winterland in front of 5,000 people. Johnny finishes the gig with `Ever get the feeling you've been cheated?'.

### 17 January 1978

It's official the Sex Pistols have split up with just over two years between first and last gigs ... R.I.P. Johnny flies to New York, Paul Cook and Steve Jones fly to Rio. They have an appointment with Ronnie Biggs, the train robber. The film is back on again, retitled `the Great Rock'n'Roll Swindle'.

# A Brief History

**June 1978**

The release of `No one is Innocent/My Way', the results of the last few months with Ronnie Biggs in Rio and Sid Vicious' recording and filming in Paris. It will reach Number 8 in the Charts.

**October 1978**

Sid and Nancy are packed off to New York. Sid plays Max's Kansas City Club in New York with Mick Jones (Clash) and a couple of New York Dolls (see `Bootleg Bible' chapter).

**11 October 1978**

Nancy Spungen is found dead in the Chelsea Hotel, New York. Sid is arrested, accused of murder.

**December 1978**

Malcolm McLaren who is still putting the finishing touches to the film appears in court against John Lydon (Rotten) over monies owed and rights to name, etc. This court case will continue for over ten years before it is resolved. Lydon & Co will win over Malcolm, claiming the £1 million prize money.

**1 February 1979**

Sid is out on bail.

**2 February 1979**

Sid found dead due to overdose of Heroin.

**February 1979**

Sid Vicious' version of `Something else' is released. It sells over 380,000 copies; the best selling `Pistols' single, it rises the Charts to Number 3.

**February 1979**

`The Great Rock'n'Roll Swindle' double LP is released. What should be the accompaniment soundtrack to the film will (due to legal actions) be in the shops a full nine months before the film is seen.

**March 1979**

`Silly thing' single is released featuring Steve Jones on vocals, the flip side `Who killed Bambi' which was the working title for the film features Ten Pole Tudor on vocals and lyrics by Vivienne Westwood. It will reach Number 6 in the UK Charts.

**June 1979**

`C'mon Everybody', another Eddie Cochran classic, is released again with Sid Vicious taking vocal duties. It will reach Number 3 in the Charts.

# A Brief History

### July 1979

`Some Product: Carri on' LP is released, an LP made up of interview material; reaches Number 6 in the Charts.

### October 1979

`The Great Rock'n'Roll Swindle' film is finally premiered nine months after its soundtrack LP. This must be a record in itself. To mark the occasion, the title track is released with `Rock Around the Clock', both from the film and both sung by Ten Pole Tudor. They will reach Number 21 in the UK Charts despite problems with the sleeve artwork (see Full Story later in book).

### December 1979

Release `Sid Sings' LP (see Full Story later in book) nearly a year after his death. It reaches No 6 in the UK Charts.

### February 1980

The Greatest Hits Package `Flogging a dead horse' is released. It will peak at 23 in the Album Charts.

### June 1980

`I'm not your stepping stone', an early Pistols' demo of the Monkees' tune tarted up for single release. It will reach Number 21 in the UK Charts.

### September 1980

`Who killed Bambi' credited to Ten Pole Tudor with the Sex Pistols is released. The second time this track is on 7" (double A side of `Silly thing' single) and will officially be the Sex Pistols' final single.

The barrel truly being drained until it's time to release them all again.

### Lesson No 11 Milk your product.

### P.S. NEVER TRUST A HIPPIE.

# Anarchy in the UK

**Anarchy in the UK/
I wanna be me**

UK 7" EMI (2566)
Release Date - 26/11/1976
Sleeve - Plain Black Sleeve
Label - Black and red lettering on cream background; standard EMI label

First 5000 run came in plain black sleeve. These mis-credit Chris Thomas as producer of the B-side 'I wanna be me'.
Demo version shown here.

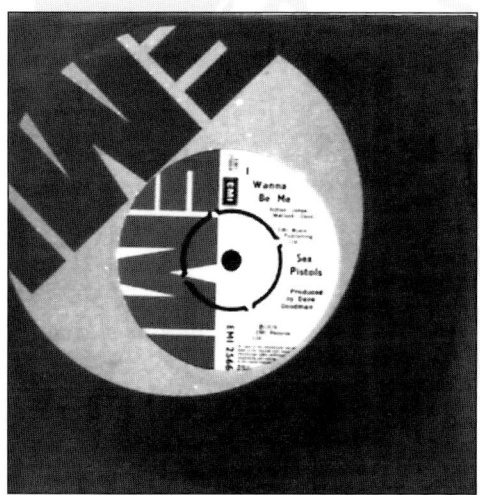

After initial run the above problem is rectified and Dave Goodman was given his production credit on B-side. This version was issued in the standard EMI company sleeve, shown here.

**The Original Acetate**

Shown here on the old style Abbey Road label
Label - Gold and black writing on blue background

# Anarchy in the UK

**Anarchy in the UK/ I wanna be me**

German 7" EMI Electrola (1C 006-06294)
Release Date - 11/1976
Sleeve - Pink and white lettering; b/w photo
Label - Black and red lettering on cream background

**Anarchy in the UK/ I wanna be me**

Dutch 7" EMI (5C 006-06294)
Release Date - 11/1976
Sleeve - Black and white lettering; b/w photo
Label - Black and red lettering on white background

**Anarchy in the UK/ I wanna be me**

Belgium 7" EMI (4C 006-06294)
Release Date - 11/1976
Sleeve - White, brown and black lettering on brown background
Label - Black and red lettering on orange background

The three classic `Anarchy' sleeves, released the same time as UK. All three credited Chris Thomas as producer of the B-side `I wanna be me', so all were withdrawn. Since the Sex Pistols and EMI parted company soon afterwards, they were never re-released.

# Anarchy in the UK

**Anarchy in the UK/
I wanna be me**

Promotional Australian 7" EMI (11334)
Promo Release Date - 11/1976
Sleeve - Red and white lettering on red background; EMI Australia sleeve
Label - Red and black lettering, blue `A', on cream background

**Anarchy in the UK/
I wanna be me**

Australian 7" EMI (11334)
Release Date - 11/1976
Sleeve - Red lettering on red background; EMI Australia sleeve
Label - White lettering on black background

**Anarchy in the UK/
I wanna be me**

New Zealand 7" EMI (2566)
Release Date - 1976
Sleeve - EMI company sleeve
Label - Red and black lettering on cream background

Both the Australian Promotional and issue copies mis-credited Chris Thomas with the B-side production and were withdrawn. The New Zealand issue had the correct production credits. Chris Thomas A-side/Dave Goodman B-side.

# Anarchy in the UK

**Anarchy in the UK/ I wanna be me**

French 7" Barclay (640 112)
Release Date - 7/1977
Sleeve - Black lettering on b/w background
Label - White lettering on black background

**Anarchy in the UK/ I wanna be me**

French 12" Barclay (740 501)
Release Date - 7/1977
Sleeve - Black lettering; b/w sleeve
Label - White lettering on black background

**Anarchie pour L'UK/ Anarchy in the UK**

French 7" Barclay (640 162)
Release Date - 3/1979
Sleeve - White, yellow and red lettering on black background
Label - White lettering on black background

Malcolm McLaren signed the Sex Pistols to Barclay Records for a 2-year period which covered territories France, Switzerland, Zanzibar and Algeria on 6 May 1977. This turned out to be a clever move as he could apply pressure to UK releases by releasing a record in France knowing full well it would be heavily imported to the UK.

# Anarchy in the UK

Back Sleeve

**Anarchy in the UK/ No Fun**

UK 7" Virgin (VS 609)
Release Date - 1983
Sleeve - Plain black front side; black and white lettering backside
Label - Black and white lettering on black background

A

B

**{A}**
**Anarchy in the UK/ No Fun/Emi**

UK 12" Virgin (609-12)
Release Date - 1983
Sleeve & Label:- As above

**{B}**
**Anarchy in the UK/ No Fun/EMI**

Mexican 12" Virgin (SL-7099)
Release Date - 1983
Sleeve & Label:- As above

This 1983 release saw Virgin releasing `Anarchy' for the first time as a 7". Using the plain bag idea (EMI release), it was released in many territories like this and also came as a 3" CD release in the UK. Same design as above.

**Anarchy in the UK/ I wanna be me**

UK 7" Virgin (VS 1431)
Release Date - 9/1992
Sleeve - Black lettering on red, black and white background
Label - Black lettering on silver background

The 1992 release of `Anarchy' to promote the `Kiss this' compilation came in a nice Jaime Reid sleeve style taken from the `Anarchy' flag shot.

# God Save the Queen

**God Save the Queen/ No Feelings**

UK withdrawn 7" A&M (AMS 7284)
Manufacture Date - 3/1977
Sleeve - Yellow and white lettering on black background; A&M company sleeve
Label - Black lettering on grey background; A&M standard label design

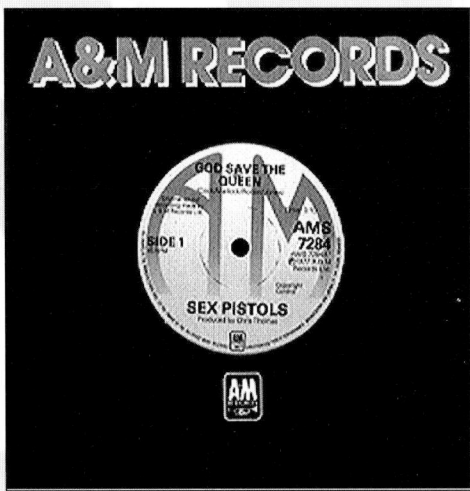 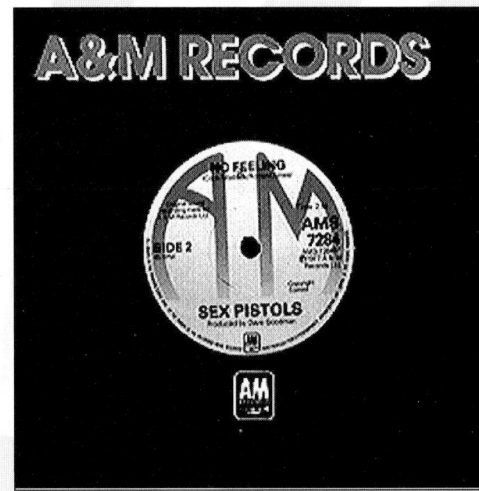

The legendary A&M version of `God Save the Queen'. Only a few survived the 25,000 pressed, as all copies were ordered to be destroyed after the Sex Pistols' contract was terminated after only seven days with the label.
**Not released.** Chris Thomas production credit A-side  Dave Goodman production credit B-side

**God save the Queen/ Did you no wrong**

UK 7" Virgin (VS 181)
Release Date - 5/1977
Sleeve - Silver and blue background
Label - Silver lettering on blue background

 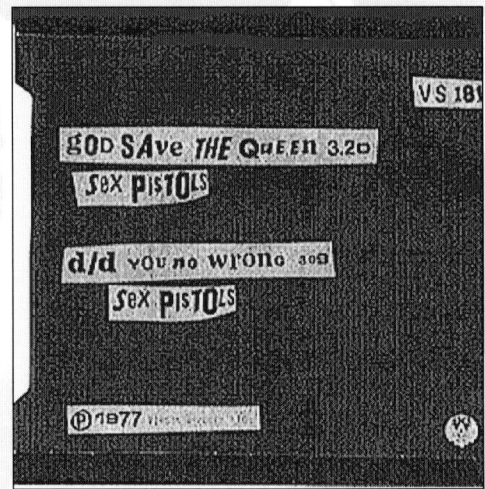

Virgin Records put this unique label design (both sides shown here) on the Sex Pistols' first release for the label and Rush released this classic track in time for the Jubilee celebrations

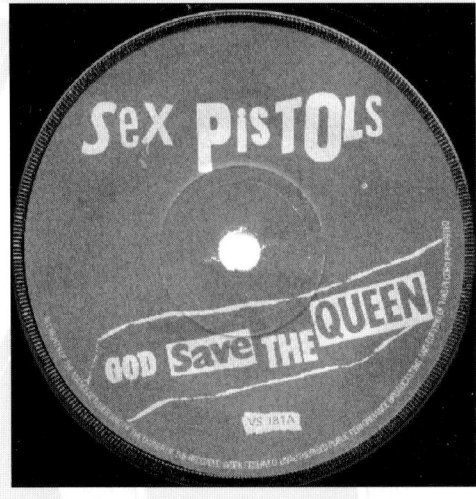 

# God Save the Queen

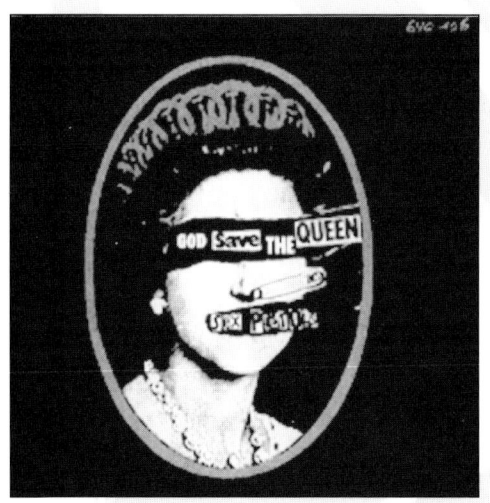 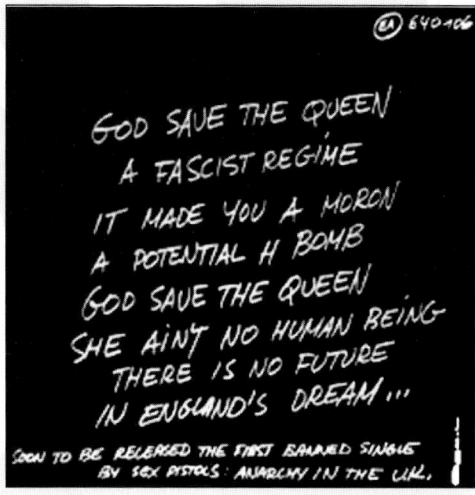

**God Save the Queen/
Did you no wrong**

French 7" Barclay (640 106)
Release Date - 5/1977
Sleeve - Front side silver and blue; backside silver lettering on black background
Label - White lettering on black background

Due to record label changes in the UK, this was the first Sex Pistols release in France. Notice the subtle changes in sleeve design, the safety pin added to Queen's nose and a lighter shade of blue background on front, while the back sleeve carries some of the songs' lyrics. Label design shown here was to remain constant on all French Barclay releases

**God Save the Queen/
Did you no wrong**

Spanish 7" Virgin (11308-A)
Release Date - 5/1977
Sleeve - Black and white sleeve
Label - The Spanish release came with two different labels - the old Virgin type label and the newer design of black lettering on blue background

The Spanish release had the same sleeve as the UK except in black and white instead of blue and silver. As Virgin were changing their label design in the UK, this affected other countries at different times.

# God Save the Queen

**God Save the Queen/
Did you no wrong**

German 7" Virgin (S11308)
Release Date - 1977
Sleeve - Same as UK except record comes out top of sleeve
Label - Black lettering on b/w background

The German release came with one of the old style Virgin labels.

**God Save the Queen/
Did you no wrong**

Japanese 7" Columbia (YK-90-AX)
Release Date - 1977
Sleeve - Blue and silver insert; both sides shown here
Label - Silver lettering on blue background

This label design and colouring was standard for all Japanese Sex Pistols Columbia releases.

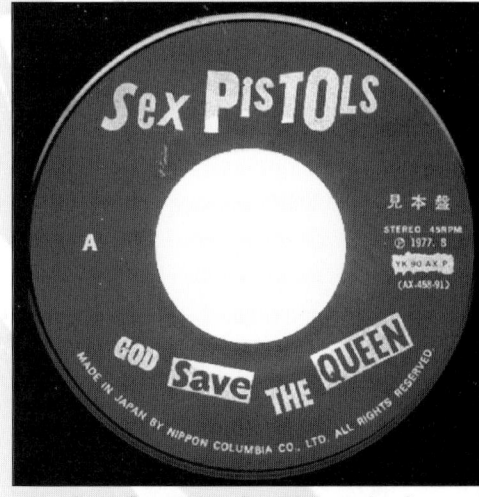

This was the first Sex Pistols release in Japan.

# God Save the Queen

**God Save the Queen/
Did you no wrong**

Australian 7" Wizard (ZS 176)
Release Date - 1977
Sleeve - Same as UK but a darker blue
Label - Pink and black lettering on blue speckled background

All original Sex Pistol releases came out on the Wizard label in Australia.

**God Save the Queen/
Did you no wrong**

New Zealand 7" (VS 181)
Release Date - 1977
Sleeve - Purple background; white design
Label - Black lettering on blue background (shown bottom left this page)

The New Zealand sleeve reduced the Queen's image on front sleeve and the background colour was more purple compared to the UK's blue colour.

**God Save the Queen/
Did you no wrong**

New Zealand 12" (VS 18112)
Release Date - 1977
Sleeve - Company sleeve
Label - Side One Black lettering on green background Side Two Black lettering on red background

# God Save the Queen

**God Save the Queen/
Did you no wrong**

Indian 7" West (8)
Release Date - 1977
Sleeve - Blue background; white design
Label - Black lettering on pink, yellow and green background

One of the strangest releases GSTQ Hits India, with the nice addition of `Punk Rock' written front top left of sleeve, with the added attraction of this weird label ??

**God Save the Queen/
Did you no wrong**

Mexican 7" Virgin (11-308)
Release Date - 1977
Sleeve - Same as UK design
Label - Black lettering on white background; Virgin emblem colour design

Nice old style label design with Mexican titles.

# God Save the Queen

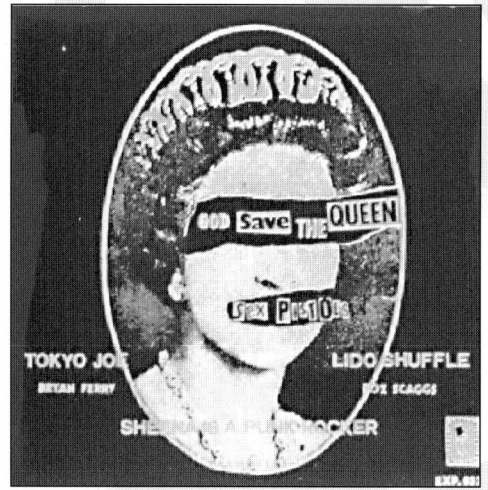 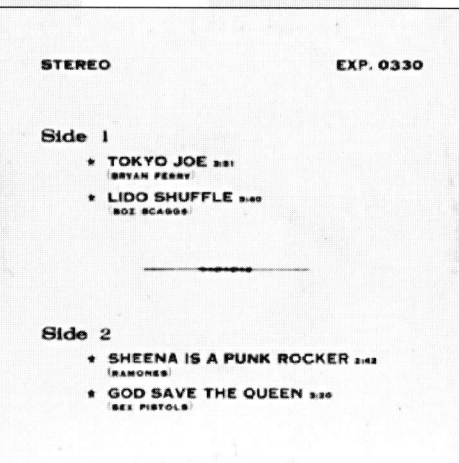

**God Save the Queen**
Thailand 7" EP Express Songs Limited (EXP 0330)
Release Date - 1977
Sleeve - Silver lettering on blue background
Label - Full colour design

4 Artists on EP:
Sex Pistols- God Save the Queen
Ramones-   Sheena is a Punk Rocker
Bryan Ferry- Tokyo Joe
Boz Scaggs- Lido Suffle

Thailand 7" records normally come out as EPs with odd couplings by different bands. Probably by other artists popular at that same time of release. This release having the double header for Punk collectors with having the Ramones on it as well.

**God Save the Queen/ Did you no wrong**
South African 7" INTERPAH (PD 1471)
Release Date - 26/9/1977
Sleeve - Silver and blue sleeve (darker blue than UK sleeve)
Label - Black lettering on b/w background

Cover looks same as UK but when put next to each other the South African one is a much darker blue. Nice old style label shown here and back cover shown with INTERPAH writing bottom right of back sleeve.

# God Save the Queen

**God Save the Queen/
Did you no wrong**

Brazilian 7" Virgin (6079-202)
Release Date - 1977
Sleeve - Blue and white lettering on blue background
Label - Black lettering on light and dark blue background

This rare Brazilian release with its `Best "Punk Rock" Group No 1 England' strip across the front sleeve and spray can style writing gives it a very distinctive look.

**God Save the Queen/
Did you no wrong/**

Don't give me no lip child
UK 3" CD Virgin (CDT 37)
Release Date - 12/1988
Sleeve - Gatefold 3" cardback/black lettering on blue and grey background

The 3" CD never really took off and only found few releases with groups. The Sex Pistols only had this one and Anarchy (3" CD 1985) in their catalogue. Included here for oddity factor ??

# Pretty Vacant

**Pretty Vacant/ No Fun**

UK 7" Virgin (VS 184)
Release Date - 7/1977
Sleeve - Black and white
Labels - a) black lettering on blue background (some with push-out middle); b) black lettering on green background (1 side) and red background (2 side)

**Label A**

**Label B**

As the label design was changing, Pretty Vacant UK had two label types (A and B shown)

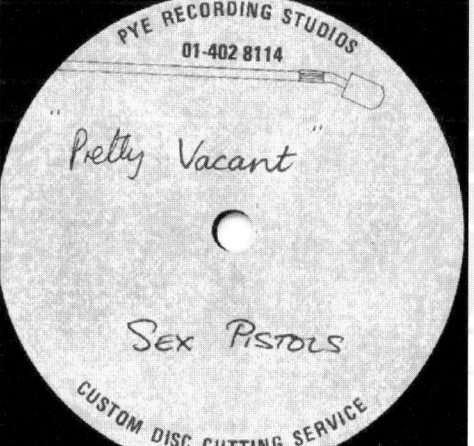

**Original Pretty Vacant**
Acetate cut at Pye Studios

# Pretty Vacant

**Pretty Vacant/
No Fun**

French 7" Barclay (640 109)
Release Date - 6/1977
Sleeve - Black and white picture
Label - White lettering on black background

Again, Barclay were quick off their toes and the French release hit the streets before the UK release. The situationist buses which appear on the reverse side of the UK sleeve are on the front of the French sleeve.

**Pretty Vacant/
No Fun**

German 7" Virgin (11331 AT)
Release Date - 1977
Sleeve - Black and white sleeve
Label - Black lettering on black and white background

The German front sleeve is an upside down version of the U.K. sleeve. Pretty Vacant written on top of sleeve lighter in shade than UK and record comes out of top of sleeve. The German back sleeve shown here is reversed - black buses on white background.

**Pretty Vacant/
L'anarchie pour Le UK**

German 7" Virgin (105 191)
Release Date - 1979
Sleeve - Colour picture
Label - Black lettering on silver background

This was taken from the soundtrack of a German film `Klassen Feind' and released in 1979. Note B side says `L'Anarchie' pour Le UK but plays `Anarchy in the UK', not the French accordion version.

# Pretty Vacant

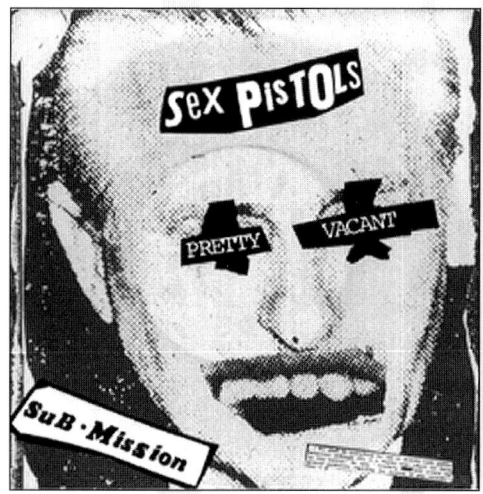 

**Pretty Vacant/ Sub-mission**
USA 7" Warner Bros (WBS 8516)
Release Date - 1977
Sleeve - Black and white lettering on yellow and green background
Label - Black lettering on white background

This was first USA release. It also came as mono/stereo `Pretty Vacant' promo, same sleeve. The reverse of the sleeve is an angry letter sent to the label. The front cover is Mr Angry himself.

**Pretty Vacant/ Sub-mission**
Canadian 7" Warner Bros (WBS 8516)
Sleeve - Company sleeve
Label - Black lettering on colour background

The same coupling of songs was released in Canada with this colourful label.

# Pretty Vacant

**LABEL A**
**Pretty Vacant/
No Fun**

Greek 7" Virgin (2097 942)
Release Date - 1977
Label - Black lettering on white background; push-out centre

**LABEL B**
**Pretty Vacant/
No Fun**

Italian 7" Virgin (VIN 45011)
Release Date - 1977
Sleeve - B/w, same as UK sleeve
Label - Black lettering on white background

Both the Greek and Italian releases use a variation of the old Virgin label. Also both countries mis-credit Chris Thomas with production of `No Fun' B-side.

**Pretty Vacant**

Thailand EP7" Express Songs Records (EXP 0342)
Release Date - 1977
Sleeve - White and pink lettering; colour picture sleeve
Label - Black and white lettering on colour background

Artists on EP:
Sex Pistols `Pretty Vacant'
The Jam `All Around the World'
The Saints `This Perfect Day'
Dave Edmonds `I knew the Bride'

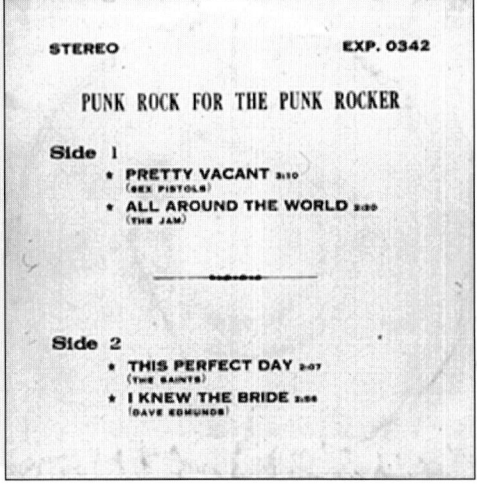

Thailand's EPs normally come out with different groups on one EP. On this occasion, they used the Jam UK sleeve for `All Around the World' as a back-drop.

# Pretty Vacant

All Australian original Sex Pistols releases came out on Wizard label.

**Pretty Vacant/
No Fun**

Australian 7" Wizard (ZS184)
Release Date - 1977
Sleeve - Black and white, same as UK
Label - Pink and black lettering on blue speckle background

**Pretty Vacant/
No Fun**

New Zealand 7" Virgin (VS 184)
Release Date - 1977
Sleeve - Black and white picture
Label - Side 1 Black lettering on green background.
Side 2 Black lettering on red background.

The New Zealand sleeve is a still from a video of the Sex Pistols live at `The Screen on the Green'. This also made up part of the promo poster `Dance with the Sex Pistols' for the `Pretty Vacant' single.

**Other release:-Pretty Vacant**
New Zealand 12" Virgin (VS 18412) in custom sleeve and label
(see G.S.T.Q. New Zealand 12")
Release Date - 1977

# Pretty Vacant

**Pretty Vacant/
No Fun**

Japanese 7" Columbia (YK-94-AX)
Release Date - 1977
Sleeve - Black and white insert, both sides shown here
Label - Silver writing on blue background

The second Japanese Sex Pistols release came as many Japanese singles do - Columbia custom bag and insert.

Magazine Cover

**Pretty Vacant/
I wanna be me**

UK free record with Spiral Scratch Magazine
Release Date - 1988
Sleeve - White inner bag
Label - Black lettering on silver background

This came out with No. 4 Spiral Scratch Magazine.
A-side is 1976 Dave Goodman demo of `Pretty Vacant'.
B-side actually plays `Seventeen' Dave Goodman demo, not `I wanna be me'.

**Pretty Vacant/
No Feelings**

UK 7" Virgin (VS 1448)
Release Date - 11/1992
Sleeve - Maroon and yellow colouring
Label - Black lettering on silver background

Virgin brought this sleeve up to date by putting Princess Diana on the front side and Fergie on the back side. Also came as a 12" in purple/ green sleeve with demo versions of No Feelings/ Satellite/ Sub-mission, as well as two CD single formats.

# Holidays in the Sun

**Holidays in the Sun/ Satellite**

UK 7" Virgin (VS 191)
Release Date - 10/1977
Sleeve - Colour sleeve
Label - Black lettering on blue background

This sleeve was withdrawn after a travel company complained it was taken straight off one of their brochures. It had been and then modified by Jamie Reed, the man responsible for all Pistols' artwork. Still, 50,000 copies had already passed through the tills before it was stopped.

**Holidays in the Sun/ Satellite**

French 7" Barclay (640 116)
Release Date - 1977
Sleeve - Colour sleeve
Label - White lettering on black background

Same as the English sleeve with the addition of `nice sleeve' written on bottom front of sleeve.

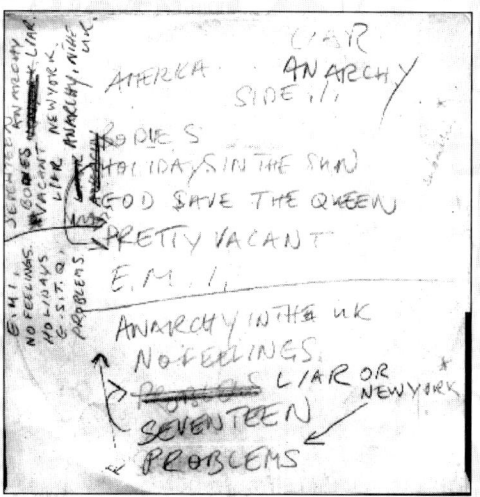 

**Holidays in the Sun**
original acetate

It's interesting to see the bag the acetate came in as it shows the changing of the order of `Never Mind the Bollocks' LP track listing. Must have been cutting the LP same time as this single.

# Holidays in the Sun

### Holidays in the Sun/ Satellite

Italian 7" Virgin (VIN 45013)
Release Date - 1977
Sleeve - Red lettering on black and white photo
Label - Black lettering on white background

Great picture sleeve. A still from the `God Save the Queen' video. Nice old Virgin label design.

### Holidays in the Sun/ Satellite

Japanese 7" Columbia (YK-97-AX)
Release Date - 1977
Sleeve - Colour sleeve
Label - Silver lettering on blue background

Insert

Same sleeve as UK with the addition of Cat No/price written in top right hand corner. This time the Japanese release came with a proper sleeve plus insert which promoted the LP `Never Mind the Bollocks' on one side and had the lyrics of A/B sides on the other.

### Holidays in the Sun Thailand EP

Release Date - 1977
Sleeve - Colour picture front
Label - Colour label
Artists on EP
Sex Pistols -   Holidays in the Sun
Status Quo -   Rocking all of the world
Joe Cocker -   Don't let me be misunderstood
Crown Heights Affair -   Boogie on up.

### Holidays in the Sun - other releases

Australia 7" Wizard (25-191)
Release Date - 1977

New Zealand 7" Virgin (VS 191)
Release Date - 1977

New Zealand 12" Virgin (VS 19112)
Release Date - 1977
12" came in custom sleeve same as `God Save the Queen NZ 12".

Thailand EPs normally come with different groups on one EP. Luckily on this occasion, they've used a colour shot of the Sex Pistols for the cover.

# Submission/New York

**Submission/
New York**

French 7" Barclay (640137)
Release Date - 10/1977
Sleeve - Black and white sleeve
Label - White lettering on black background

French only release. Apparently was to be a UK release but Malcolm pushed it out in France first, so heavily imported and was left at that. Cover shot is a still from `God Save the Queen' video.

# Lentilmas Flexi

**Lentilmas Flexi - a seasonal offering to you from Virgin Records**

(Christmas freebie flexi disc)
Promotional Release - 12/1977
33 rpm

It was always rumoured that this flexi had some Sex Pistols involvement, albeit just Steve Jones and Paul Cook. Sent out to press from Virgin Records, the cover is an Xmas card with fictional stories on front. Signed inside by Virgin Press. The flexi contains seasonal messages.

# No One is Innocent / My Way

**No One is Innocent (a punk prayer by Ronald Biggs)/ My Way**

UK 7" Virgin (VS 220)
Release Date - 6/1978
Sleeve - Blue and yellow lettering, colour picture
Label - Black lettering on white background

First post Rotten Pistol '45' train robber Ronnie Biggs takes lead vocals. Much confusion over the title of this track. Malcolm McLaren initially wanted to call it 'Cosh the Driver' but was stopped by Virgin UK. A step too far. The 12" of same track was called 'The Biggest Blow', but Malcolm got his way with his French allies, Barclay (see next page). The title 'No One is Innocent' is an old libertarian phrase.

**The Biggest Blow (a punk prayer by Ronald Biggs)/ My Way**

UK 12" Virgin (VS 22012)
Release Date - 6/1978
Sleeve - Black and white
Label - Black lettering on white background

Some copies came with an interview after A-side (Matrix No VS 22012 A3) with Steve Jones/Paul Cook and Ronald Biggs various questions like 'Where's the Money', etc., etc.

**12" Singles Promotional Album**

In-store play - not for resale
Promo only release - 1978

The 'My Way' 12" track found its way on this 12" promo LP featuring Virgin acts such as Ruts/ Japan/ Human League/ XTC, etc., etc.

# No One is Innocent / My Way

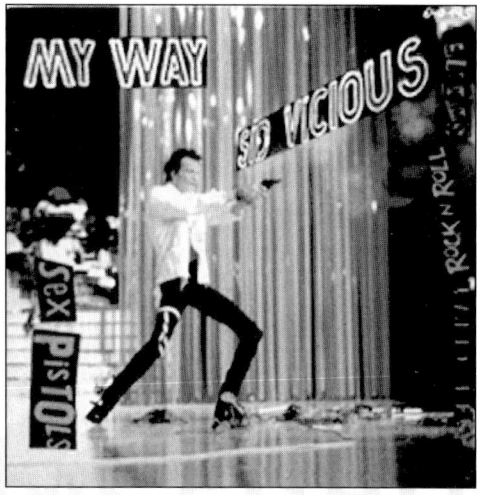 

**My Way/
Cosh the Driver**

French 7" Barclay (640 145)
Release Date - 6/1978
Sleeve - Gold and silver lettering, colour picture
Label - White lettering on black background

The French release saw the UK release being flipped over making the more popular `My Way' the A-side. The sleeve is similar to the British except the yellow lettering became gold and the colours were brighter. Also Malcolm got his way and called the flip side `Cosh the Driver'. Some copies exist crediting `Cosh the Driver' to Sid Vicious.

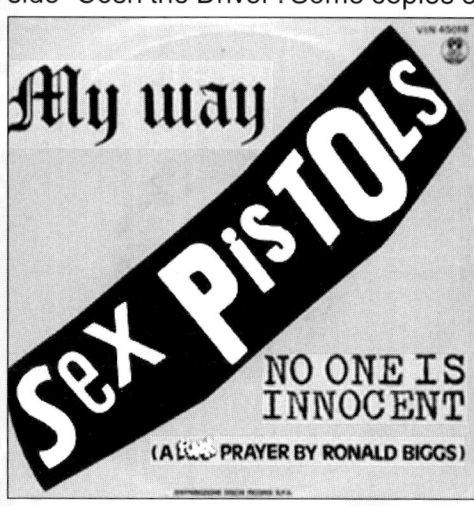

**No One is Innocent (a punk prayer by Ronald Biggs)/
My Way**

Italian 7" Virgin (VIN 45018)
Release Date - 1978
Sleeve - Black and yellow lettering on yellow background
Label - Black lettering on blue background

This classic Italian sleeve with its pastiche of the `Never Mind the Bollocks' sleeve turned out, surprisingly, to be the only one to do so.

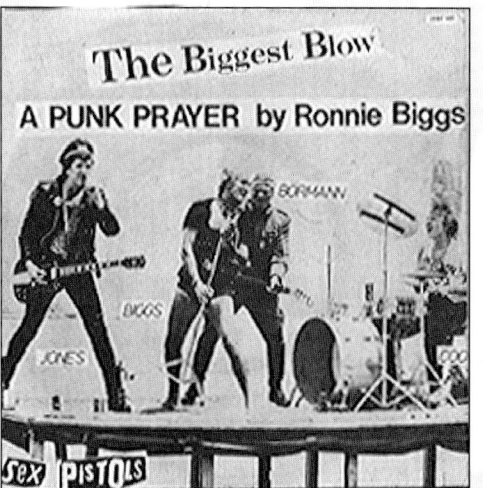 

**The Biggest Blow/
My Way**

Greek 7" Virgin (2097 961)
Release Date - 1978
Sleeve - Black and white
Label - Black lettering on white background

This rare release used the 12" UK sleeve/ titles - the only country to do so.

# No One is Innocent /My Way

**No One is Innocent/
My Way**

Japanese 7" Columbia (YK-109-AX)
Release Date - 1978
Sleeve - Yellow and blue lettering, colour picture
Label - Silver lettering on blue background

This Japanese release came with a proper sleeve and insert; one side promoting the LP plus three previous 7" singles, the other side the lyrics of A/B side.

**No One is Innocent/My Way - other releases**

Dutch 7" Virgin (15707)
Release Date - 1978
Sleeve - White and pink lettering, pink wash over UK sleeve

Australian 7" Wizard (ZS-190)
Release Date - 1978

Australian 12" Wizard (ZS-12-190)
Release Date - 1978
Sleeve - same as UK 12"; came in clear vinyl first, then black vinyl

New Zealand 7" Virgin (VS 220)
Release Date - 1978

New Zealand 12" Virgin (VS 22012)
Sleeve - Virgin custom sleeve (see G.S.T.Q. New Zealand)

# Something Else / Friggin' in the Riggin'

Sid Vicious takes over lead vocal on A-side. Steve Jones sings a bawdy sea chant traditional song on the flip side. Some mis-pressings around with A-side playing `Silly Thing' sung by Paul Cook. Back side of UK same as French front side below.

The French release saw the tracks being flipped over making `Friggin" the A side. Also, the Swastika is blacked out from Sid's T-shirt on back side.

**Something Else/ Friggin' in the Riggin'**
UK 7" Virgin (VS 240)
Release Date - 1979
Sleeve - Colour sleeve front shown on left, back cover shown below (French front release)
Label - Side One Picture label (same as GR&R Swindle LP Sleeve) Side Two Black lettering on green background (first run came with b/w labels)

**Friggin' in the Riggin'/ Something Else**
French 7" Barclay (640 159)
Release Date - 2/1979
Sleeve - Colour
Label - White lettering on black background

## OTHER RELEASES

**Something Else/ Friggin' in the Riggin'**
German 7" Virgin
Release Date - 1978

**Something Else/ Friggin' in the Riggin'**
Australian 7" Wizard (ZS 305)
Release Date - 1978

**Something Else/ Friggin' in the Riggin'**
New Zealand 7" Virgin (VS 240)
Release Date - 1978

**Something Else/ Friggin' in the Riggin'**
Italian 7" Virgin (VIN 45023)
Release Date - 1979
Sleeve - Colour same as UK
Label - Colour same as UK

The Italian release also left off the Swastika on Sid's T-shirt.

# Silly Thing

**Silly Thing/
Who Killed Bambi**

UK 7" Virgin (VS 256)
Release Date - 3/1979
Sleeve - Front Red, blue and white Back Colour, yellow circle on black background
Label - A-side Colour GR&R Swindle LP cover B-side Black lettering on purple background

Steve Jones sings the A-side; Tenpole Tudor sings the B-side.

**Who Killed Bambi/
Silly Thing**

French 7" Barclay (640 160)
Release Date - 3/1979
Sleeve - Colour
Label - White lettering on black background

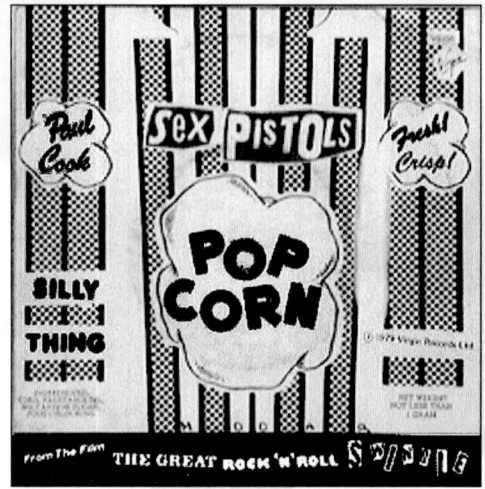

Not only did the French release reverse the UK 45, it uses Paul Cook's version of `Silly Thing' from GR&R Swindle LP. Notice just Paul Cook's name on sleeve (UK Paul & Steve). Also, French release includes the European standard grams/ 28.3/ 02, bottom right on back sleeve shown here.

**Silly Thing/
Anarchy in the UK**

Portuguese 7" Virgin (VV-45 009ES)
Release Date - 1979
Sleeve - Front Pink and white lettering, colour pictures Back Black and white
Label - Black lettering on blue background (like Virgin UK)

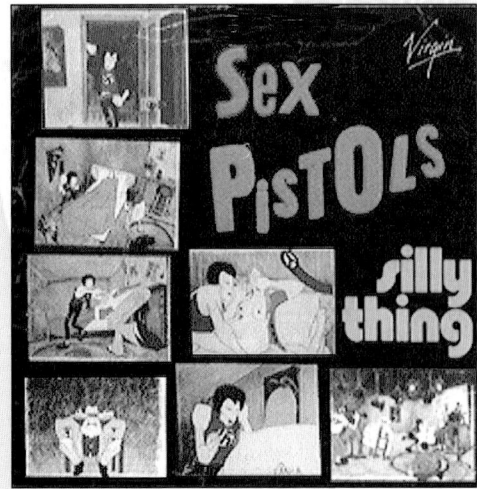 

Great sleeve using stills from GR&R Swindle. It's B-side says `Anarchy in the UK' but actually plays `Anarchie pour l'UK'. The French accordion version from GR&R Swindle.

# Silly Thing

**Silly Thing/
Something Else**

Japanese 7" Columbia (YK-122-AX)
Release Date - 1979
Sleeve - Columbia bag and colour insert
Label - Silver lettering on blue background

This Japanese release has Paul Cook's version of `Silly Thing' and Sid Vicious' `Something Else', two UK singles together. Also, they reverted back to `insert' sleeve with this release.

## OTHER RELEASES

### Silly Thing/Who Killed Bambi

German 7" Virgin (100-104)
Release Date - 1979
Sleeve - Same as UK, record comes out top of sleeve
Label - Black lettering on green background one side, red background on other side
Steve Jones on vocals.

### Silly Thing/Who Killed Bambi

Australian 7" Wizard (ZS311)
Release Date - 1979

### Silly Thing/Who Killed Bambi

New Zealand 7" Virgin (VS 256)
Release Date - 1979
Sleeve - Front As French release, Paul Cook name only . Back Circle around Bambi's head blue
Label - Black lettering on green background one side, red background on other side
Paul Cook on vocals.

# You Need Hands

**You Need Hands/God Save the Queen (Symphony)**
French 7" Barclay (640 161)
Release Date - 3/1979
Sleeve - Yellow and red lettering, colour picture
Label - White lettering on black background

Malcolm takes over lead vocals on this French only release on the A-side, and also the vocal version 'God Save the Queen (Symphony)' on B-side. Great sleeve, again using stills from GR&R Swindle film with the classic Malcolm Declares 'Never Trust a Hippie' on the back sleeve

# Heritage EP

**Sid Vicious - Heritage EP**
French 12" Barclay (740.509)
Release Date - 1979
Sleeve - Colour sleeve
Label - White lettering on black background

This French 12" only release featured all three of Sid's lead vocals 'My Way', 'Something Else'/'C'mon Everybody'. It came in a Jamie Reid artwork sleeve showing a Sid Vicious action man in a coffin with Sid looking on. The Swastika was again removed from Sid's T-shirt.

# C'mon Everybody

 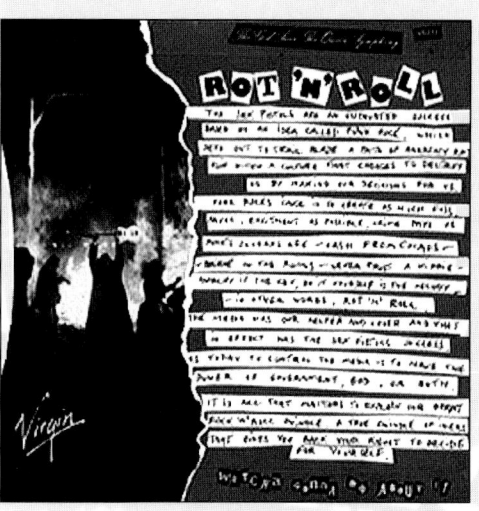

**C'mon Everybody/God Save the Queen (Symphony)/ Watcha Gonna Do about It**

UK 7" Virgin (VS 272)
Release Date - 6/1979
Sleeve - Colour Sleeve
Label - Colour one side GR&R Swindle LP cover; other side black lettering with yellow background

Sid Vicious sings another Eddie Cochran classic with `God Save the Queen (Symphony)' instrumental version and added extra 1.55 seconds of `Watcha Gonna Do about It', which was removed from the GR&R Swindle LP.

## OTHER RELEASES

**C'mon Everybody/
God Save the Queen (Symphony)/
Watcha Gonna Do about It**

German 7" Virgin (100 179)
Release Date - 1979
Sleeve - Same as UK, record comes out top of sleeve

**C'mon Everybody/
God Save the Queen (Symphony)/
Watcha Gonna Do about It**

Australian 7" Wizard (ZS 313)
Release Date - 1979

# The Great Rock'n'Roll Swindle

### The Great Rock'n'Roll Swindle/
### Rock Around the Clock

UK 7" Virgin (VS 290)
Release Date - 10/1979
Sleeve - **Front** Blue/green credit card on black background **Back** Red lettering, colour pictures on black background
Label - Colour GR&R Swindle LP cover one side - (A) other side black lettering on purple background; (B) other side black lettering on yellow background

Tenpole Tudor sings vocals on both sides of this single which caused an uproar at the time with `American Express' getting the sleeve withdrawn due to the plagiarising of their card on the cover. Two editions of this single hit the streets; the first with the purple background label (A) being just the A/B side, the second followed shortly afterwards with yellow background label (B). This contained a taped message after the `GR&R Swindle' track, from American Express to Virgin Records expressing their displeasure.

### The Great Rock'n'Roll Swindle/
### Rock Around the Clock

German 7" Virgin (VS 100 916-100)
Release Date - 1979
Sleeve - **Front** Pink/yellow/red lettering on black background **Back** Same as UK
Label - Black lettering on green background one side, red background other side

# (I'm not your) Stepping Stone

**(I'm not your) Stepping Stone/
Pistols Propaganda**
UK 7" Virgin (VS 339)
Release Date - 6/1980
Sleeve - Colour sleeve
Label - A-side GR&R Swindle
LP cover colour B-side Black
lettering on lime green
background

The A-side features a 1976 Dave Goodman demo.
Nice sleeve using a still from GR&R Swindle cartoon section. This was also to be used for GR&R Swindle when it became a single album. The B-side is a radio advert type talk over with excerpts of tracks.
Some mis-pressings can be found of this single, one where the band's version of the Who's `Substitute' plays on the A-side, and some where a `Gillian' track plays on the A-side.

### OTHER RELEASES

**(I'm not your) Stepping Stone/
Pistols Propaganda**
German 7" Virgin (100-339 100)
Release Date - 1980

**(I'm not your) Stepping Stone/
Pistols Propaganda**
New Zealand 7" Virgin (VS 339)
Release Date - 1980

**(I'm not your) Stepping Stone/
Pistols Propaganda**
New Zealand 12" Virgin (VS 33912)
Release Date - 1980
Sleeve - Custom sleeve (see G.S.T.Q. New Zealand 12")

# SEX PISTOLS 6 PACK

**God Save the Queen/
Pretty Vacant**

Sex 1-1 Pistols Pack
Label - Black lettering on yellow background

**Holidays in the Sun/
My Way**

Sex 1-2 Pistols Pack
Label - Black lettering on purple background

**Something Else/
Silly Thing**

Sex 1-3 Pistols Pack
Label - Black lettering on green background

The Sex Pistols' pack of 6 x 45 singles came out in December 1980 coupling the A-side of singles together, plus two new Cook/Jones tracks `Black Leather/Here we go Again'. The 6-singles came in a plastic wallet that folded down to reveal the six singles. The pink flap at the top read `Sex Pistols Special Price Limited Edition Sex 1

# Sex 1 Release: 12/1980

**C'mon Everybody/
The Great Rock'n'Roll Swindle**

Sex 1-4 Pistols Pack
Label - Black lettering on brown background

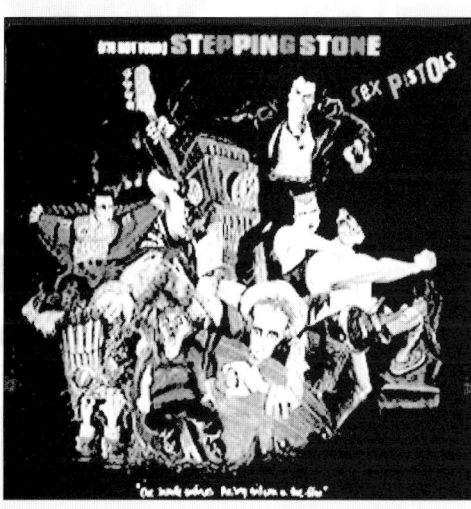

**(I'm not your) Stepping Stone'
Anarchy in the UK**

Sex 1-5 Pistols Pack
Label - Black lettering on orange background

The original artwork was used, but where necessary due to a withdrawn/band sleeve the artwork for that side was changed. See Holidays in the Sun/The Great Rock'n'Roll Swindle/Anarchy in the UK, and in the case of Black Leather/Here We Go Again, new artwork was made. All sleeves full colour shots both sides.

**Black Leather/
Here We Go Again**

Sex 1-6 Pistols Pack
Label - Black lettering on red background

1) This pack also came out in France with French labels and `Six 45 Tours' pink sticker on front of plastic wallet
2) These six singles came out in Greece later in a yellow 7" box (Never Mind the Bollocks looking cover)
VG-008-VG-013

# The Heyday Cassette

**The Heyday Cassette**
**UK Cassette Factory Fact 30**
Release Date - 10/1980
Cassette - Gold colour
Label - Red lettering on black background
Cover - Black plastic pouch reading in red lettering "The Sex Pistols - The Heyday - Fact 30"

A cassette only release - it featured interviews on
**Side One** Sid Vicious/Steve Jones by Judy Vermoral 1977 and
**Side Two** Paul Cock/Johnny Rotten and Malcolm McLarens Grandmother.

# Who Killed Bambi

**Who Killed Bambi/**
**Rock Around the Clock**
UK 7" Virgin (VS 443)
Release Date - 9/1981
Sleeve - Colour sleeve, yellow circle around Bambi on black background
Label - Black lettering on red background

The final official Sex Pistols 7" was credited to Ten Pole Tudor with the Sex Pistols. Eddie Ten Pole Tudor singing the A & B cuts. Who Killed Bambi ???

# Sub-mission / No Feelings

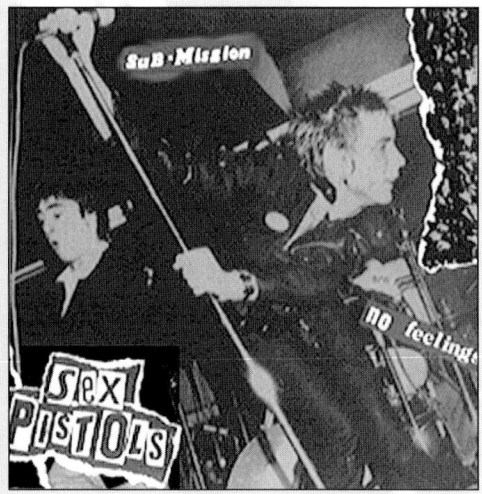 

**Sub-mission/
No Feelings**
UK 7" Chaos (Dick 1)
Release Date - 1/1985
Sleeve - White with gold surround lettering on pink and blue background
Label - Black lettering on white background

These tracks were recorded by Dave Goodman between 13 and 30 July 1976. These 7"s came as a limited edition of 5,000 copies, half on yellow vinyl, half on pink vinyl. The `No Feelings' track is the version that was on the B-side of the A&M withdrawn single "God Save the Queen"

**The Acetate "Sub-mission"**
Cut at Abbey Road Studios
Notice the newer design of label, light and dark blue in colour

# Sub-mission/ Anarchy in the UK

**Sub-mission/
Anarchy in the UK**

UK 12" Chaos (Cartel 1T)
Release Date - 1/1985
Sleeve - White and black lettering, full colour sleeve
Label - Black lettering on white background

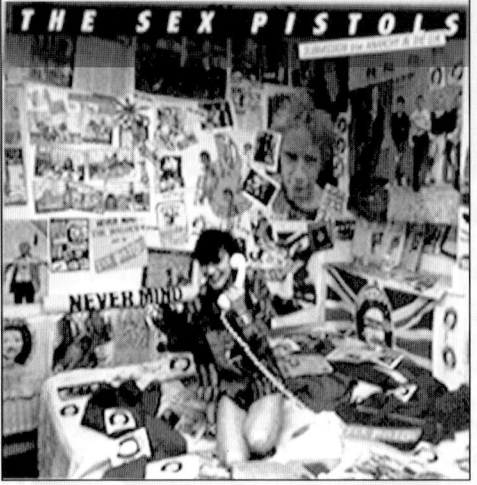 

These tracks were recorded between 13 and 30 July 1976 by Dave Goodman. They were released on seven different colour vinyls - yellow, blue, red, white, green, clear and pink - and about 12,000 were made. There is also a promo copy 12" shown here.

**Sub-mission - 1-sided Promotional 12"
Promo release date -
8 October 1984**

Label - Black lettering with red `A' on white background
Sleeve - Plain white inner sleeve only

**The Acetate Cut of `Anarchy' in the UK**

Cut at Abbey Road Studios
Label - Light and dark blue background

# UK 7" Single Sleeves

Anarchy in the UK page 13

G.S.T.Q. A&M withdrawn page 18

G.S.T.Q. Virgin page 18

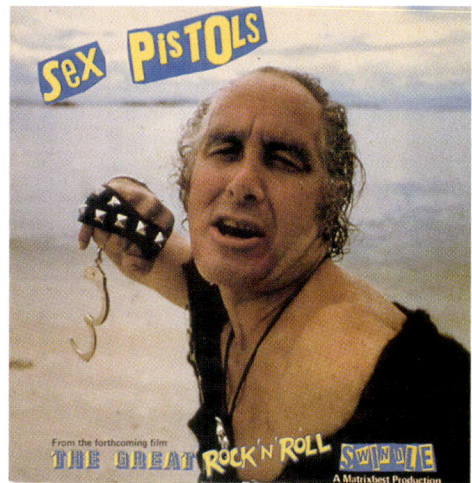

Pretty Vacant page 25

Holidays in the sun page 31

No one is innocent page 34

Something else page 37

Silly thing page 38

C'mon everybody page 41

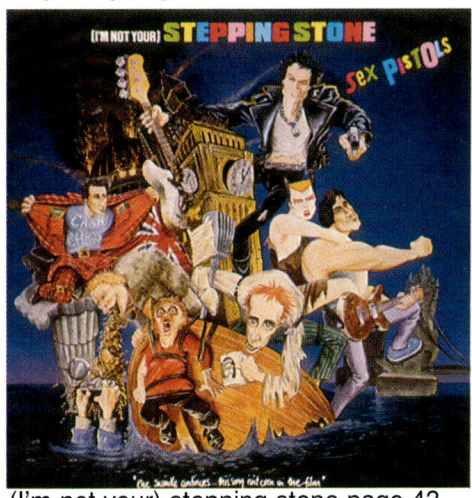

Great R&R swindle page 42

(I'm not your) stepping stone page 43

Who killed Bambi page 46

# Rare foreign 7" Sleeves

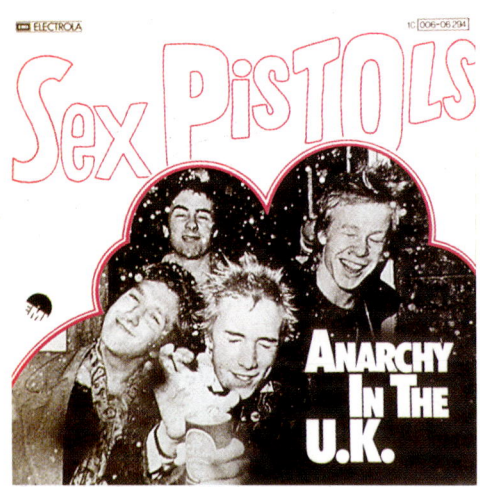
Anarchy in the UK (german) page 14

Anarchy in the UK (dutch) page 14

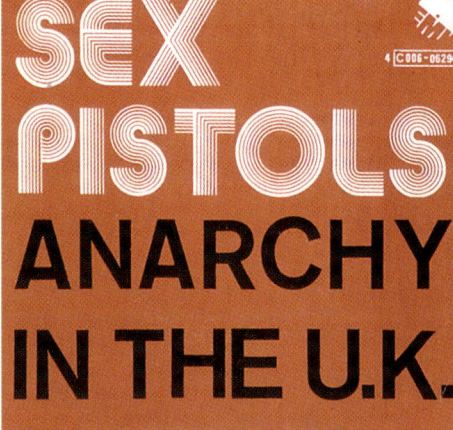
Anarchy in the UK (belgian) page 14

G.S.T.Q. (mexican) page 22

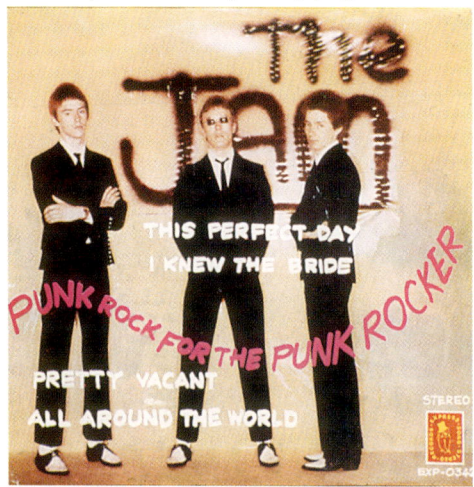
Pretty Vacant (thai) page 28

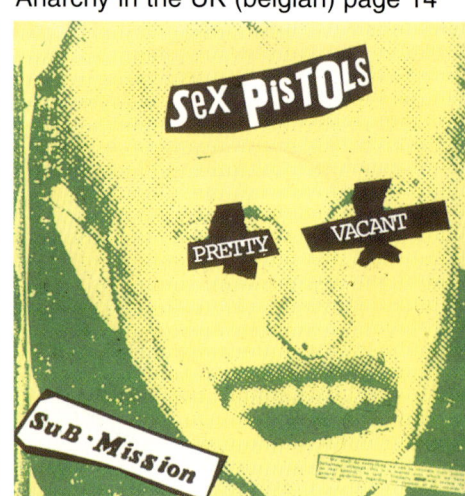
Pretty Vacant (USA) page 27

Pretty Vacant (german) page 26

Holidays in the sun (italian) page 32

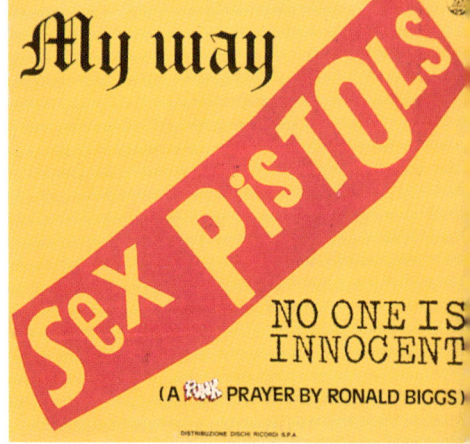
No one is innocent (italian) page 35

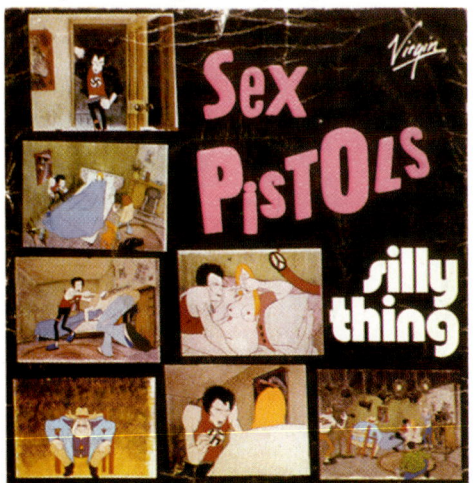
Silly thing (portuguese) page 38

Silly thing (japanese) page 39

You need hands (french) page 40

# Album Sleeves

N.M.T.B. page 49

N.M.T.B. Picture Disc page 56

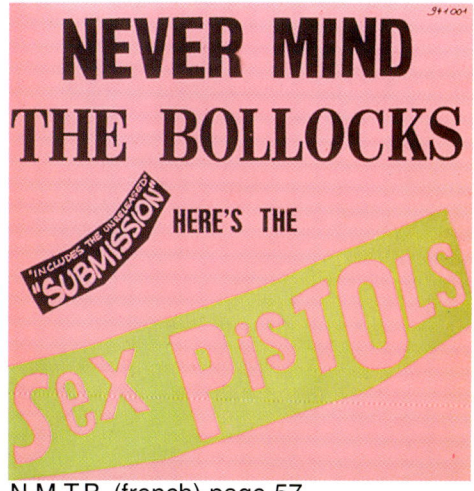

N.M.T.B. (french) page 57

Great R&R swindle Double LP page 62

Great R&R swindle Single LP page 67

Great R&R swindle (french) page 62

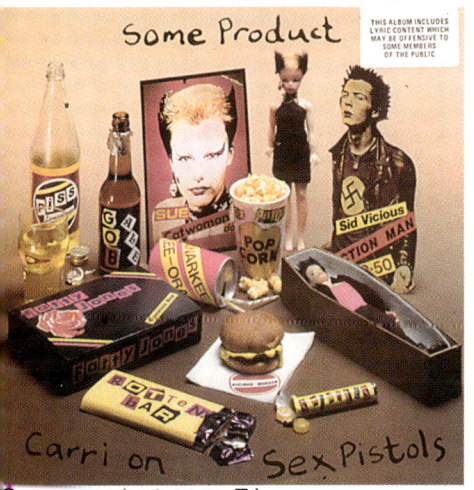

Some product page 71

Tho very best of (japanese) page 72

Flogging a dead horse page 73

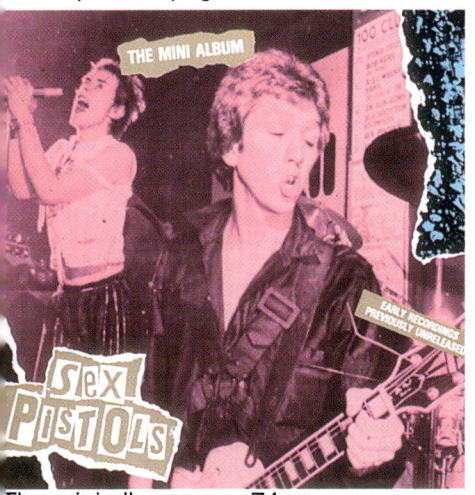

The mini album page 74

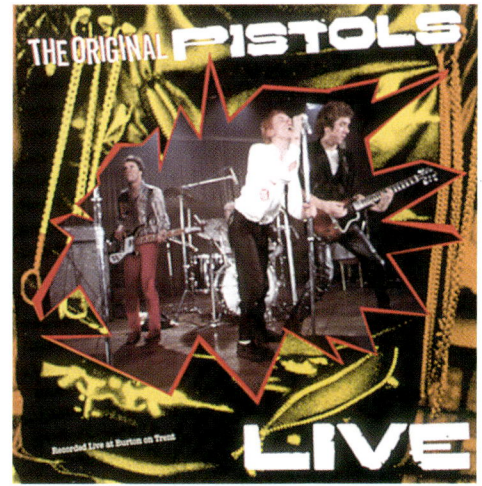

The original pistols live page 76

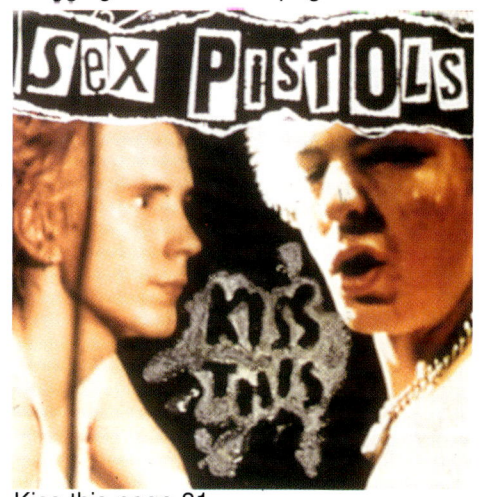

Kiss this page 81

# Bootleg bible album sleeves

No future UK page 83

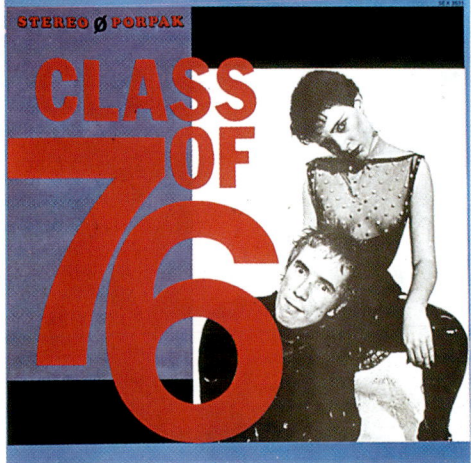
Class of '76 page 83

St. Albans bash page 84

Nashville page 84

100 Club punk festival page 85

Indecent exposure page 85

Bad boys in Sweden page 86

Bad boys page 86

Tour of scandinavia page 87

Sex Pistols Sweden page 87

Anarchy in the USA page 89

Vicious Burger page 90

'Never Mind the BOLLOCKs'

# NEVER MIND THE BOLLOCKS

HERE'S THE

**Sex Pistols**

The Full Story

# 'Never Mind the BOLLOCKS'

## The Whole BOLLOCKS

'Never Mind the Bollocks' was the subject of many changes right up until the last moment, with various sleeve changes, mainly to the back side track listing order.

Its original working title 'God Save the Sex Pistols' got as far as cover proofs, but was dropped in favour of 'Never Mind the Bollocks' which itself led to many problems. Many shops were warned they could face prosecution under the 1899 law regarding obscene advertising for displaying LPs and posters with the word 'Bollocks'.

The manager of Virgin records in Nottingham was to be taken to court on this very point. Still they won the court case proving the word 'Bollocks' had been used from the year 1,000 and appeared in many venerable books since. As they say, no publicity is bad publicity. As far as the track listing and eventual release, the story runs like this:

## Never Mind the BOLLOCKS - Four Different UK Versions

The running order of 'N.M.T.B.' was changing daily. But when it went to pressing the LP, eleven tracks were agreed on. But in Pistols' style at the eleventh hour, the group insisted on the inclusion of 'Submission (12th track) being on the LP.

The copies already run were possibly going to be scrapped, but due to import copies arriving from France (see N.M.T.B. - the French Connection story in this chapter), panic set in. Would everybody buy the heavily imported French album version for the extra track. Which was already on the streets, with a printed sleeve reading :-

**N.M.T.B. includes the unreleased 'Sub-mission track'.**

So plan two went into action to release the initial copies of the 200,000 run and add a 1-sided 7" containing 'Sub-mission' track.

# 'Never Mind the BOLLOCKS'

## Never mind the Singles ... 10 Tracks!!

One story floating around was that Virgin being a hippy label didn't want an LP release to be filled with 7" single releases as N.M.T.B. was.

1) Anarchy in the UK
2) God save the Queen
3) Pretty Vacant
4) Holidays in the Sun
5) Sub-mission/New York was a French single release also

The other story which gives this tale more substance was when N.M.T.B. hit the streets, within an hour it was banned from Boots, Woolworths and W H Smiths, which in England at the time were the 3 major record outlets.

A plan was put together to reissue the album straight away deleting:-

(a) the singles,

(b) the offending tracks that caused the ban.

So these chain stores would stock the LP.

Making the album 10 tracks long with the inclusion of `Satellite' only available up until now as the B-side of `Holidays in the Sun', the track listing would have read as follows:

### Side 1

1) Bodies
2) New York
3) Sub-mission
4) Liar
5) EMI

### Side 2

6) Problems
7) No feelings
8) Seventeen
9) Satellite
10) Anarchy in the UK

As you can see in this chapter, the idea went as far as re-cutting the album, but somewhere along the line and powers that be, this never saw fruition.

# 'Never Mind the Bollocks'
## Four Different UK Versions

**So the versions were:-**

**Version 1**
The 11-track LP with a 7" single and full colour poster, shrink-wrapped together, rush released a week earlier than planned. Note the back cover of N.M.T.B. with this edition reads 11 tracks with no `Sub-mission'.

**Version 2**
This came with the re-cut album containing twelve tracks (with Sub-mission). A thousand of these got out with a plain pink back cover, no track listings.

**Version 3**
Then came N.M.T.B. with printed sleeve with twelve tracks printed on back cover including `Sub-mission' track.

**Version 4**
Three months later in January 1978 came the picture disc version of N.M.T.B. in pink die cut sleeve with tracks written in black and white in order, as opposed to scattered on back cover.

### Track Listing of N.M.T.B. Version 1   (11 Tracks)

**Side 1**
1) Holidays in the Sun
2) Liar
3) No feelings
4) God save the Queen
5) Problems

**Side 2**
6) Seventeen
7) Anarchy in the UK
8) Bodies
9) Pretty Vacant
10) New York
11) EMI

### Track Listing of N.M.T.B. Versions 2, 3 & 4   (12 Tracks)

**Side 1**
1) Holidays in the Sun
2) Bodies
3) No feelings
4) Liar
5) God save the Queen
6) Problems

**Side 2**
7) Seventeen
8) Anarchy in the UK
9) Sub-mission
10) Pretty Vacant
11) New York
12) EMI

# 'Never Mind the Bollocks'
## Other Strange Stories

To add to the confusion, over the years the track listings on the back sleeve have varied from reprint to reprint. Some have read:

1) `Satellite' instead of `Bodies'

2) `Sub-mission' fails to appear on some copies

3) `Belsen was a gas' appears on some copies

4) Some have `Liar' written twice and `Belson was a gas', but no `Holidays in the Sun' or `God save the Queen'

But rest assured that track listings and running order of the LPs themselves remain constant around the world except for the USA and Canada editions which for some reason changed the order of the last two tracks of Side 1.

**USA/ Canada**                **UK Edition**

Track 5    Problems            Track 5    God save the Queen

Track 6    God save the Queen  Track 6    Problems

The other exception to the rule is France ...

# 'Never Mind the BOLLOCKS'

## The French Connection

As we stated earlier, Malcolm McLaren used his French deal with Barclay to great effect. When not getting his way at home with UK label Virgin, he would often force their hand by releasing something in France (next door to UK) knowing full well it would be heavily imported forcing a UK release.

This strategy was put to good use when Virgin were dithering over a release date and Malcolm, then pushing for the admission of `Sub-mission' (excuse the pun!) used his trump card and got the album released in France straight away. Not a point often made was:-

**The first N.M.T.B. to hit the streets was the French edition.**

The French track listing ran different to the UK, moving around `Liar', `Problems' and `Sub-mission' as shown below.

**French Track Listing**

**Side 1**

1) Holidays in the Sun
2) Liar
3) No feelings
4) God save the Queen
5) Problems
6) Sub-mission

**Side 2**

6) Seventeen
7) Anarchy in the UK
8) Bodies
9) Pretty Vacant
10) New York
11) EMI

**English Track Listing**

**Side 1**

1) Holidays in the Sun
2) Bodies
3) No feelings
4) Liar
5) God save the Queen
6) Problems

**Side 2**

7) Seventeen
8) Anarchy in the UK
9) Sub-mission
10) Pretty Vacant
11) New York
12) EMI

But as the French track listing came first, who's to say this is not the correct one; in fact :-
**The official track listing of N.M.T.B.**

Maybe ... play it and see ... C'est la vie.

# 'Never Mind the Bollocks'
## 4 Versions

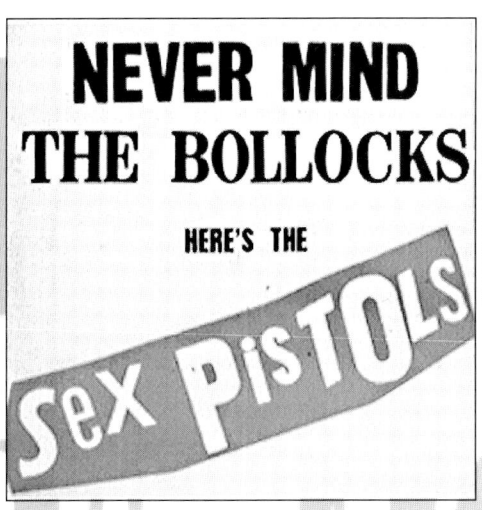

**Version 1**
**Never Mind the Bollocks**
UK LP Virgin (V 2086)
Release Date - 10/1977
Sleeve - Front Black and yellow lettering on yellow and pink background Back Black lettering on pink background

**Version 1** came with a 1-sided 7" single (VDJ 24) of `Sub-mission' plus poster, a montage of symbols for the tracks on LP with sticker sealed.
Back cover does not list `Sub-mission'; it's not on this LP release, just on the 7" 11 tracks.

Picture of LP, colour poster and single

A) Original LP label
   Black lettering on dark blue background

B) Label 1-sided 7"
   Sub-mission
   Black lettering on light and dark blue background

55

# 'Never Mind the Bollocks'

### Version 2
**Never Mind the Bollocks**
UK LP Virgin (V 2086)
Release Date - 10/1977
Sleeve - Same front, pink **back**, no track listings

**Version Two.** 1,000 copies of LP came with just pink background, no track listings. But with sub-mission added to LP - 12 tracks.

### Version 3
**Never Mind the Bollocks**
UK LP Virgin (V 2086)
Release Date - 10/1977
Sleeve - Same front **Back** Black lettering on pink background

**Version Three.** Proper track titles now on back sleeve - 12 tracks

### Version 4
**Never Mind the Bollocks**
UK Picture Disc LP Virgin (VP 2086)
Release Date - 1/1978
Sleeve - **Front** Die cut hole for picture, black lettering with pink surround **Back** Black lettering in white boxes on pink background

**Version Four.** This came out three months later in January. Picture disc itself stage shot of group same both sides.

# "Never Mind the Bollocks"

**Never Mind the Bollocks**

UK Promotional LP Virgin (V 2086)
Promo Release Date - 1979
Sleeve - Same as UK with 12 tracks on back
Label - Black lettering on white background

N.M.T.B. came as a promotional copy with promo label shown here and the proper twelve track listing on back cover. This came out in 1979 to re-promote N.M.T.B. with release of GR&R Swindle LP.

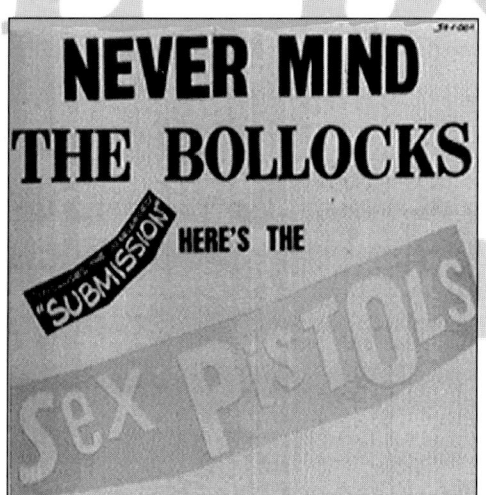

**Never Mind the Bollocks**

French LP Barclay (941 001)
Sleeve - **Front** Black and pink lettering on pink and green background **Back** Black lettering in pink and black boxes on green background

Label - White lettering on black background

This was actually the first N.M.T.B. edition to hit the streets (see Story in this section). This edition was followed by reverting the sleeve to its standard colour (same as UK black/yellow & pink); the back cover was plain pink - no track listing (Cat No Barclay 941001)

**Never Mind the Bollocks**

Acetate shown here
Pye Studios

The acetate cut of the possible alternative N.M.T.B. (see Story Never mind the Singles...10 tracks in this chapter).

# 'Never Mind the BOLLOCkS'

**Never Mind the Bollocks**
USA LP Warner Bros (BSK 3147)
Release Date - 1977
Sleeve - Black and pink lettering on pink and green background
Label - Black lettering on white background

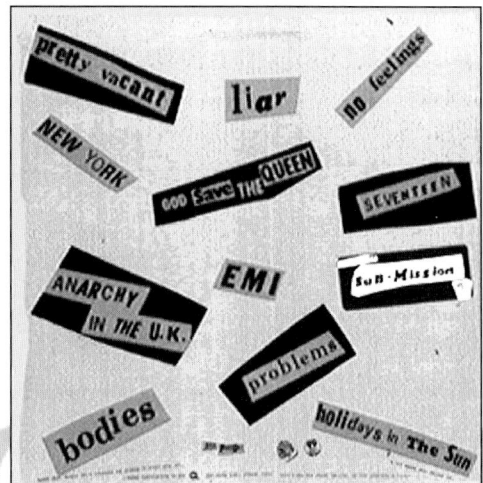

The USA edition came with a nice inner sleeve shown here. Blue and white background.

The USA and Canada editions look the same (see Story this chapter).

**Never Mind the Bollocks**
Japanese LP Virgin/Toshiba EMI (25VB-1068)
Release Date - 1978
Sleeve - Front Same as UK front
Back Same as picture disc UK
Label - One side black lettering on red background; other side black lettering on green background

Shown here is a promotional copy of this Japanese release which comes with inner gatefold sheet with lyrics. N.M.T.B. also came out on Columbia Japan (YX-7199), released 1977.

# 'Never Mind the BoLLOCkS'

### Never Mind the Bollocks
German LP Virgin (25 593XOT)
Release Date - 1977
Sleeve - Same as UK, tracks on back
Label - Black lettering on green background

This German release has a nice old style variation to the Virgin label. It comes with the Version 1 style English sleeve tracks on back, but not reading `Sub-mission' although it is on the LP

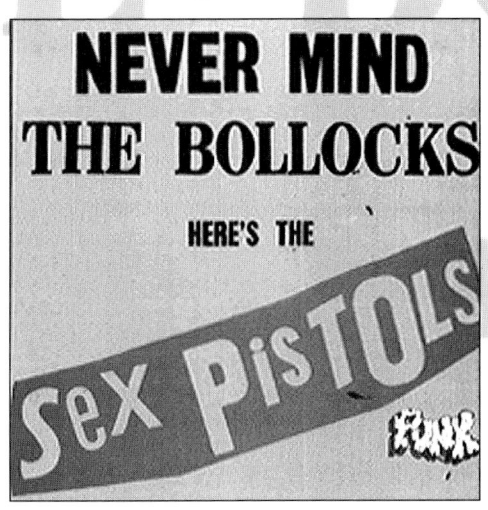

### Never Mind the Bollocks
Italian LP Virgin (VIL 12086)
Release Date - mid 1980s
Sleeve - As UK, tracks on back not reading `Sub-mission', but is on LP
Label - Side1 Black lettering on red background Side 2 Black lettering on green background

This Italian release looks nice with it's `Punk' written bottom right on front sleeve. It has a later style label so must have been an 80s release.

### Never Mind the Bollocks
Argentinean Promo LP Virgin (TLP 60169)
Release Date - 1986
Sleeve - As UK
Label - Side1 Black lettering on red background Side 2 Black lettering on green background

Strange to see an Argentinean release, never mind a promo. This came out in 1986, but is still very scarce to find.

# 'Never Mind the BOLLOCKS'

**Other Never Mind the Bollocks Releases**

Australian Wizard (ZL 225)
Release Date - 1977
Same sleeve as UK/Wizard label

New Zealand Virgin (V 2086)
Same sleeve as UK

Canada Warner Bros (KBS 3147)
Same as USA

Brazil Virgin
Release Date - 1978

South African Virgin

Greece Virgin (2933710)

Portuguese Virgin (VV-33.012)
80s release

Australian Virgin (red vinyl/green vinyl)
90s release

Never Mind the Bollocks' was first released in October 1977. It came out at the same time in various countries - France, Germany, Japan, USA, Australia/New Zealand to name but a few, and came out later in various other countries, and was still being released in different areas in the 1980s. Most countries have been hit by a N.M.T.B. bug by now, but it's still evolving, ie. Australia issued coloured vinyls of the LP in the 1990s ... it goes on ...

# The Great Rock'n'Roll Swindle

The Whole Story

# The Great Rock'n'Roll Swindle

## The Whole Story

Malcolm McLaren again used the Sex Pistols' French Record deal with Barclay to push forward release dates for the soundtrack LP. By this stage, the group as we know it had split up, a lot of their money, and money owed was tied up in the `Great Rock'n'Roll Swindle' project. A lot of last minute changes were happening. Track running orders, new tracks to be included. The LP itself was made up of odds and ends, demos and some new material recorded by Paul Cook and Steve Jones with various singers as Johnny Rotten (John Lydon) wanted nothing to do with the project.

Due to these various delays, Virgin again (as they were with `Never Mind the Bollocks' LP) were beaten to the presses and the French release was hitting the streets.

The initial 10,000 copies of the LP that had been run by Virgin UK were to be destroyed due to these last minute changes, but to counteract the flood of French copies being heavily imported these were put out; this being the reason why the UK had two versions of the double LP hitting the streets at the same time.

As you can see later in this chapter as we deal with each version step-by-step, there are a lot of strange things happening- tracks on covers not matching LP track listings themselves and so on. All under the guise of: "Sorry about the incorrect track listing on sleeve - it's another swindle".

Malcolm tried to get his way with calling the `No one is Innocent' track `Cosh the Driver', but this was pulled after the initial 10,000 run credited on the sleeve only.

# The Great Rock'n'Roll Swindle

**These are the initial UK track listings for the `Great Rock'n'Roll Swindle':**

| Version 1 | Version 2 |
|---|---|

### Side 1 / Side 1

Version 1:
1) God save the Queen(Symphony)
2) Rock around the Clock
3) Johnny B Goode
4) Road Runner
5) Black Arabs Medley
6) Watcha gonna do about it
7) Anarchy in the UK

Version 2:
1) God save the Queen (Symphony)vocal
2) Johnny B Goode
3) Road Runner
4) Black Arabs Medley
5) Anarchy in the UK

### Side 2

Version 1:
8) Silly thing
9) Substitute
10) Don't give me no lip child
11) (I'm not your) Stepping Stone
12) Lonely Boy
13) Something Else

Version 2:
6) Substitute
7) Don't give me no lip child
8) (I'm not your) Stepping Stone
9) L'Anarchie pour le UK
10) Belsen was a gas (live)
11) Belsen was a gas (studio with Biggs)

### Side 3

Version 1:
14) L'Anarchie pour le UK
15) Belsen was a gas (live)
16) Belsen was a gas (studio with Biggs
17) No one is Innocent
18) My way

Version 2:
12) Silly thing
13) My Way
14) I wanna be me
15) Something else
16) Rock around the Clock
17) Lonely boy
18) No one is innocent

### Side 4

Version 1:
19) C'mon everybody
20) Emi (orch)
21) The Great Rock'n'Roll Swindle
22) You need hands
23) Friggin' in the Riggin'

Version 2:
19) C'mon everybody
20) Emi (orch)
21) The Great Rock'n'Roll Swindle
22) Friggin' in the Riggin'
23) You need hands
24) Who killed Bambi

# The Great Rock'n'Roll Swindle

The inside of the gatefold LPs where the track listings are get the tracks wrong also. This is due to sleeves already being printed, etc.

**Version 1** cover gets away with it by saying the magic words `includes' covering itself nicely.

**Version 2** cover lists `Watcha gonna do about it' but is not on LP and lists Track 7 Side 1 as `Who Killed Bambi' but LP plays `Anarchy in the UK'. The other minor differences are listed with each version in this chapter.

It's just for us to stay that in 1980 `The Great Rock'n'Roll Swindle' was reduced to a single LP release which mainly stuck to the 7" single releases for its track listing but also includes the vocal version of `God save the Queen (symphony)' even though it doesn't say on cover of record.

### The Great Rock'n'Roll Swindle
### Single LP Track Listing

Side 1

1) God Save the Queen (symphony)
2) The Great Rock'n'Roll Swindle
3) You Need Hands
4) Silly Thing
5) Lonely Boy
6) Something Else

Side 2

1) Rock Around the Clock
2) C'mon everybody
3) Who Killed Bambi
4) No one is Innocent
5) L'anarchie pour le UK
6) My Way

This track listing is consistent for all the various versions of the single LP all over the world.

# The Great Rock'n'Roll Swindle

## 3 U.K. Commercial Versions

**Version 1**
**The Great Rock'n'Roll Swindle**
UK Double LP Virgin (VD 2510)
Release Date - 2/1979
Sleeve - Colour gatefold (see notes)
Labels - Colour GR&RS picture Side 1
1st Set Black lettering on yellow background
2nd Set Black lettering on red background

This first run of 10,000 copies plays `Watcha gonna do about it', has different artwork for track listing, credits `No one is Innocent' as `Cosh the Driver' on sleeve but not on label and has just `Who killed Bambi' in red on back sleeve.

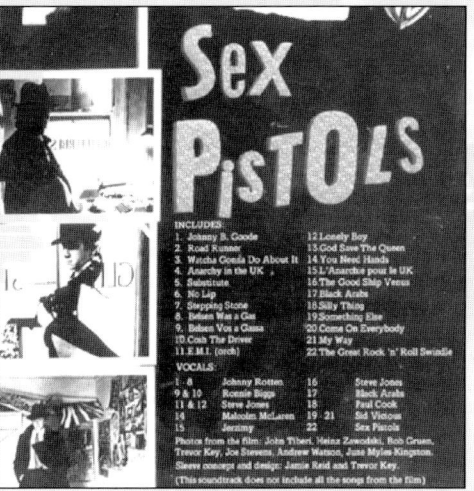

Shown here inside of gatefold LP showing original layout for track listing.
Notice the `Cosh the Driver' listed on sleeve.

Label design that ran on one side of each label. Colour.
This picture design carried on most of the single 7" releases taken from this LP set except `No one is Innocent' and `Who killed Bambi' 7"'s.

# The Great Rock'n'Roll Swindle

**Version 2**
**The Great Rock'n'Roll Swindle**

UK Double LP Virgin (VD 2510)
Release Date - 2/1979
Sleeve - Colour gatefold
 (see notes)
Labels - Same design as
 Version 1

This version does not play `Watcha gonna do about it' but credits it on sleeve. It adds `I wanna be me' demo, plus `Who killed Bambi'. Also plays a different version of `God save the Queen (symphony)' with added Malcolm McLaren vocal overdubs.

The artwork is different for track listing area. Also back sleeve carries extra writing in blue ink which originally stems from McLaren's Dickensian poster for the Huddersfield concert on Christmas Day 1977.

Shown here inside of gatefold (Version 2); notice new artwork layout for track listing area

# The Great Rock'n'Roll Swindle

**Version 3**
**The Great Rock'n'Roll Swindle**

UK Single LP Virgin (VZ 168)
Release Date - 5/1980
Sleeve - Colour (see notes)
Labels - Side 1 Black lettering on red background  Side 2 Black lettering on green background

The Great Rock'n'Roll Swindle LP was released as a single LP in 1980. Nice cartoon sleeve from film and movie stills on back.  15,000 came with a poster shown here. The tracks were cut down to mainly the singles.

**10" Promo Set for Great Rock'n'Roll Swindle Film**

4 x B/W promo pictures.
3 x inserts - (1) Interview Julian Temple; (2) Reviews; (3) Credits.

# The Great Rock'n'Roll Swindle

**French :- Two Editions**

### Edition 1
### The Great Rock'n'Roll Swindle

French Double LP Barclay (930101/02)
Release Date - 2/1979
Sleeve - Colour (see notes)
Label - Same design as UK (see notes)

This version does not play `Watcha gonna do about it' but credits it on the sleeve. Has different artwork for track listing area than both UK copies. The reverse cover has the `Shot Bambi' photo, which is bordered by various newspaper cuttings in black lettering with gold surround. This was the first GR&R Swindle LP to hit the streets!!

Shown here inside of gatefold. Notice different artwork for track listing on French edition.

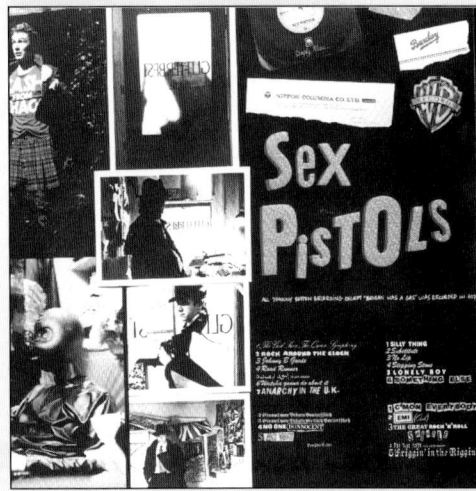

### Edition 2
### La Grande Escroquerie du Rock'n'Roll

French Single LP Virgin (202 521)
Release Date - 6/1980
Sleeve - Colour (see notes)
Label - same layout as UK single LP

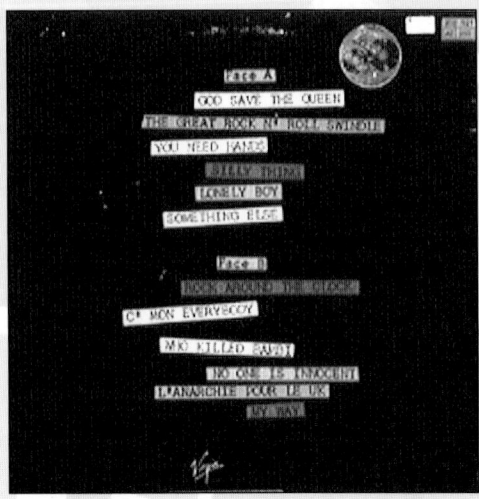

This French edition comes with great Jaime Reed artwork and movie stills. Has same track listing as UK single LP and is the only French release to be on Virgin due to the Barclay contract ending before its release.

# The Great Rock'n'Roll Swindle

**Great Rock'n'Roll Swindle**

UK Promo LP Virgin (VD 2510)
Promo Release only - 2/1979
Sleeve - Colour same as Version 2
Label - Black lettering on white background

**Insert**

Uses same sleeve as Version 2 so track listing is wrong on cover, but adds an insert shown here with correct track listing. Plays the same tracks as Version 2. Label has written on it: "Sorry about incorrect track listing on sleeve - it's another swindle".

**An original set of Acetates**
for the Double LP set

# The Great Rock'n'Roll Swindle

### The Great Rock'n'Roll Swindle

Australian Double LP Wizard (ZL 237)
Release Date - 2/1979
Sleeve - Colour same as UK Version 2
Label - Black and pink lettering on blue speckled background

The GR&R Swindle came out in Australia in 1979, as usual on the Wizard label, but with the difference that it was on multi-coloured vinyl.

### The Great Rock'n'Roll Swindle

Italian LP Virgin (VIL 12168)
Release Date - 1980
Sleeve - Same as UK (see notes)
Label - Same as UK design

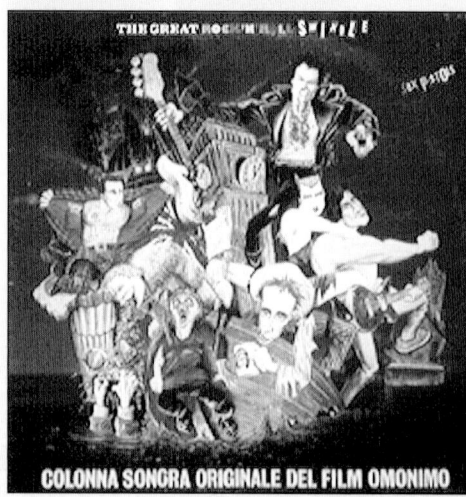

The Italian single LP release with Italian writing at base of front sleeve. "Colonna sonora originalle del film omonimo". Nice!!

### The Great Rock'n'Roll Swindle

Israel LP Virgin (V 2168)
Release Date - 1980
Sleeve - Same as UK (see notes)
Label - Same as UK design

The Israeli release with its distinctive writing bottom right of front sleeve.

As we said with `Never mind the Bollocks', the Great Rock'n'Roll Swindle continues with releases popping up everywhere, especially with the advent of CD!! Keep those cameras rolling

# Some Product - Carri On Sex Pistols

**Some Product - Carri On**
UK LP Virgin (V2)
Release Date - 7/1979
Sleeve - Colour
Label - Side 1 Black lettering on green background Side 2 Black lettering on red background

This LP is made up of interviews, radio adverts for their records, the famous Bill Grundy interview included. The cover is made up of phoney Sex Pistols products - `Fatty Jones Chocolates', `Rotten Bar', `Sex Pistols Popcorn', `Vicious Burger', etc.

The back cover shot is the sign for Chelsea Hotel in New York `The Scene of the Crime' and they have added Sid Vicious' name to the plaque.

The label for the promotional copy of this album

# The Very Best Of The Sex Pistols

**The Very Best of The Sex Pistols**

Japanese only LP Columbia (YX-7247-AX)
Release Date - 1979
Sleeve - Black and pink lettering on pink and green background
Label - Silver writing on blue background

Best of compilation release in Japan only comes with two inserts:
(A) B/W gatefold with history of The Sex Pistols in Japanese (handy!!)
(B) Pink and white two-sided insert with song lyrics in English (nice!!) but often wrong.

### Track Listing

**Side 1**

1) Pretty Vacant
2) No fun
3) Anarchy in the UK
4) I wanna be me
5) God save the Queen
6) Here we go again

**'B' Insert**

**Side 2**

6) Rock'n'Roll Swindle
7) C'mon everybody
8) Did you no wrong
9) Black leather
10) Satellite
11) Silly thing
12) My way

**'A' Insert**

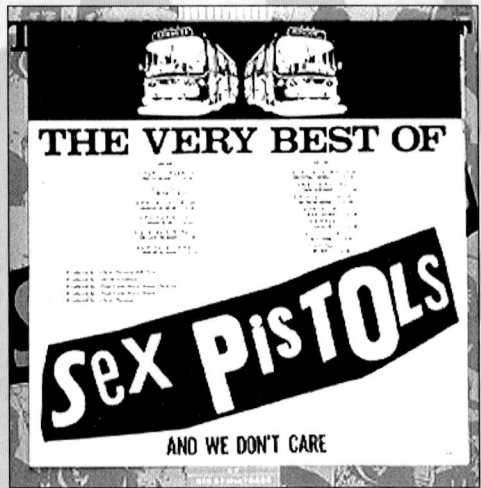

**'B' Insert**

# Flogging a Dead Horse

## Flogging a Dead Horse

UK LP Virgin (V 2142)
Release Date - 2/1980
Sleeve - Colour cover
Label - Side 1 Black lettering on red background Side 2 Black lettering on green background

This compilation was really the original UK Greatest Hits package and has a strong track listing but was cheapened by giving it the title `Flogging a Dead Horse', especially with its mock `Top of the Pops' compilation type cover.

## The Acetate Copy

this time cut at Utopia Studios

## Track Listing

### Side 1

1) Anarchy in the UK
2) I wanna be me
3) God save the Queen
4) Did you no wrong
5) Pretty Vacant
6) No fun
7) Holidays in the sun

### Side 2

8) The Biggest Blow
9) My way
10) Something else
11) Silly thing
12) C'mon everybody
13) Stepping stone
14) The Great Rock'n'Roll Swindle

# The Mini Album

**The Mini Album**
UK LP Chaos (Mini 1)
Release Date - 1/1985
Sleeve - White lettering in gold boxes on pink and blue background
Label - Black lettering on white background

This album consists of 6 demos recorded by Dave Goodman (the Group's sound engineer) between 13 and 30 July 1976. Since Dave Goodman owed the rights to these recordings, by licensing them to Chaos Records makes this an official release.

### Track Listing

**Side 1**

Submission
Seventeen
Satellite

**Side 2**

I wanna be me
Anarchy in the UK
No feelings

**The Mini Album**
Japanese LP VAP (35155-20)
Release Date - 1985
Sleeve - As UK
Label - Black lettering on white background

The mini album was released in Japan and as usual with Japanese releases comes with lyric sheet but also `The Perfect History of Sex Pistols' written in Japanese on the insert.

# The Mini Album

**Back Picture**

**`The Mini Album' Picture Disc**
Picture Disc LP Antler (Antler 37)
Release Date - 1/1986

**A - side 1st issue**

The Mini Album was reissued one year later as a picture disc. The 7th demo recorded by Dave Goodman between 13 and 30 July 1976 was held back for this release. `Pretty Vacant' was added and `I wanna be me' was taken off.

It came out as two editions -
**1 Issue** with a live group shot on one side,
**2nd issue** with the 12" cover of `Submission/Anarchy in the UK' (Chaos cartel 1).

**A - side 2nd issue**

**Track Listing**

**Side 1**

Pretty Vacant
Anarchy in the UK
No feelings

**Side 2**

Sub-mission
Seventeen
Satellite

# The Original Pistols Live

**The Original Pistols Live**
UK LP EMI Fame (FA 4131491)
Release Date - 1986
Sleeve - Colour
Label - Black and red lettering
on red and cream background

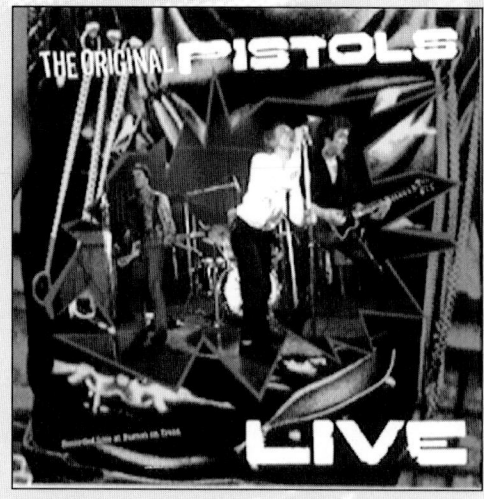

This is the legendary `Indecent Exposure' bootleg (see `Sex Pistols Bootleg Bible' chapter) which was given legitimacy by being taken up as an EMI budget release LP.

The receiver label also put out a version of this LP (RRLP 001) in 1985 adding two tracks from the Bootleg `(I'm not your) Stepping Stone' and `Sub-mission'.

**Track Listing**

**Side 1**

1) Anarchy in the UK
2) I wanna be me
3) I'm a lazy sod (seventeen)
4) New York
5) Don't give me no lip child
6) Substitute

**Side 2**

7) Liar
8) No feelings
9) No fun
10) Pretty Vacant
11) Problems

The LP is a live recording of a Sex Pistols gig at Burton on Trent on 24 September 1976.

# Better Live than Dead

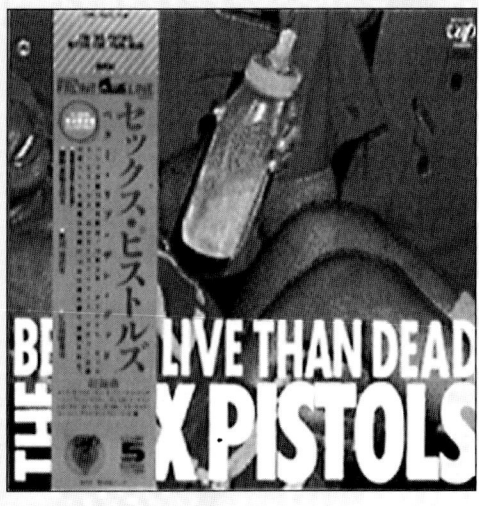

**Better Live than Dead**
Japanese LP VAP (35161-25)
Release Date - 6/1986
Sleeve - Colour
Label - Black lettering on green background

This Japanese only release consists of live Pistols tracks leased from Dave Goodman. Comes with nice packaging, insert with lyrics, plus a four track 7" EP. Label shown here.

**7"EP Label shown here.**

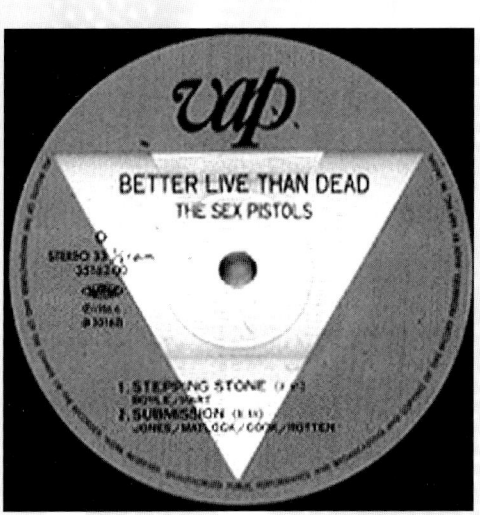

## Track Listing

| Side A | | Side B | |
|---|---|---|---|
| 1) | Liar | 6) | Problems |
| 2) | Substitute | 7) | Anarchy in the UK |
| 3) | No feelings | 8) | I wanna be me |
| 4) | No fun | 9) | I'm a lazy sod |
| 5) | Pretty Vacant | | |

## EP Track Listing

| Side C | | Side D | |
|---|---|---|---|
| 10) | Suburban kid (New York) | 12) | Stepping stone |
| 11) | Don't give me no lip child | 13) | Sub-mission |

The live gig is basically Burton on Trent in a different order + two tracks.

# The Swindle Continues

**The Swindle continues**
Japanese Double Picture Disc
LP VAP (352045-45)
Release Date - 1988
Sleeve - Die cut full colour gatefold
Insert - Orange gatefold sheet containing lyrics

Another Dave Goodman sanctioned project. Gets a Japanese only release. A lavish production, full colour gatefold containing two colour picture discs. Picture Disc One is made up of a recording session in January 1977 at Gooseberry Studios and two tracks from October 1976 at Wessex Studios.

The second picture disc is more dubious. It contains tracks recorded by and called Ex-Pistols which is definitely Dave Goodman and Glen Matlock in the studio, possibly Paul Cook?? Recorded many years later.

## Track Listing

**Sex Pistols Side**

Side A

1) No future
2) Problems
3) Pretty Vacant
4) Liar

Tracks 1-6 Gooseberry Studios

Side B

5) EMI
6) New York
7) No fun
8) Anarchy in the UK

7-8 Wessex Studios

**Ex-Pistols Side**

Side C -

1) Here we go again
2) Silly thing
3) Dancing on the Dole
4) Anarchy in the UK

Side D

5) Revolution in the classroom
6) Judging minds
7) Sex on 45
8) The Swindle continues

Side C tracks 1 & 2 Steve and Paul. The rest Ex Pistols.

The Promo of this edition carries the promo Japanese writing on the picture discs themselves.

# Party till you Puke

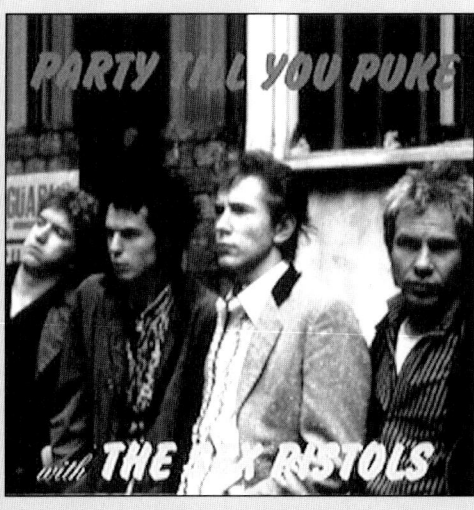

**Party till you Puke**
German LP TTE (005)
Release Date - 1989
Sleeve - Pink and yellow writing - colour picture
Label - Black lettering on yellow and white background

This LP comes in that no-mans-land of `semi official' releases but is worth the find as it contains demos of `Never Mind the Bollocks' LP recorded in 1977 at Wessex Sound Studios,

**Track Listing**

**Party Side A**

1) E.M.I.
2) Submission
3) Satellite
4) No feelings
5) Seventeen

**Puke Side B**

6) Bodies
7) New York
8) Liar
9) E.M.I. (2nd version)
10) Submission (2nd version)

# Live at Chelmsford Prison

**Live at Chelmsford Prison**
USA LP Restless (772511-1)
Release Date - 1993
Sleeve - Colour
Label - Silver lettering on black background

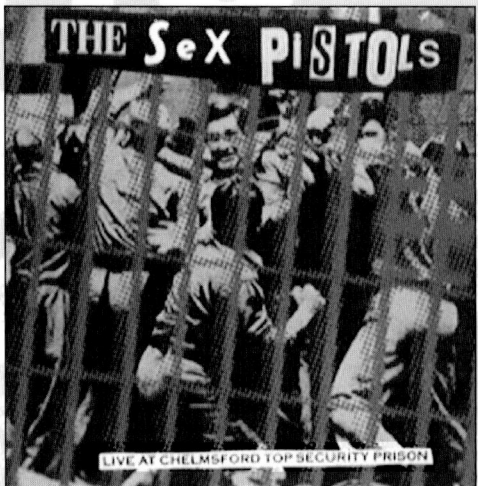

This is one of the issues of a tape rumoured to exist but stayed hidden until the 90s. Dojo also put out a version of this gig. Recorded on 17 September 1976 at Chelmsford Prison by Dave Goodman.

**Track Listing**

**Side 1**

1) Satellite
2) Submission
3) Liar
4) No fun
5) Pretty Vacant
6) Problems

**Side 2**

7) I wanna be me
8) Lazy Sod (seventeen)
9) New York
10) No lip
11) Stepping stone
12) Substitute
13) Anarchy in the Prison
14) Did you no wrong

Overdubs were added to this LP. Extra cheering, bass parts by Glen Matlock which is a pity as in its original form is a `classic' in its own right.

# Kiss This

**Front and Back Gatefold**

**Kiss This**

UK Double LP Virgin (V 2702)
Release Date - 10/1992
Sleeve - Colour gatefold
Label - black and white

This 1992 double LP compilation is basically the `Never Mind the Bollocks' LP, plus the B-sides of the first four singles, plus two cover version demos and two of the best post-Rotten songs `My Way' (Sid), `Silly Thing' (Cook/Jones). It comes in a nice gatefold sleeve, with a written interview on the inside of the gatefold with the Pistols themselves talking through each track.

## Track Listing

### Side A

1) Anarchy in the UK
2) God save the Queen
3) Pretty Vacant
4) Holidays in the sun
5) I wanna be me

### Side B

6) Did you no wrong
7) No fun
8) Satellite
9) Don't give me no lip child
10) (I'm not your) Stepping stone

### Side C

11) Bodies
12) No feelings
13) Liar
14) Problems
15) Seventeen

### Side D

16) Submission
17) New York
18) Emi
19) My Way
20) Silly thing

**Inside Gatefold**

The LP was re-mastered by Rotten/Lydon. Also came as a CD edition with fold-out poster and a limited edition (Virgin CD VX 2702) with a live bonus CD Live in Norway the `Trondheim Tape'.

# Sex Pistols Bootleg Bible:- 3 Essential 7"

**And We Don't Care**
Side One - Problems
Side Two - Pretty Vacant/No feelings
Sleeve - B/W

Chris Spedding demos Majestic Studios 1976.
German bootleg.

**Regular S.F. Hippies and assorted long hairs**
Side One - Ksan Live Report/Bodies/Holidays in the Sun
Side Two - Pretty Vacant/Anarchy in the USA
Sleeve - Yellow and black wraparound

Radio broadcast KSAN from Winterland Gig 14 January 1978. Blue vinyl.
Swedish bootleg.

**`Rotten Role' Records**
(SUK 1)
Side One - Anarchy in the USA
Side Two - Belsen was a gas
Sleeve - B/W

Live USA Tour 1978.
American bootleg.

# Sex Pistols Bootleg Bible:-

Out on the streets before `N.M.T.B.', the unofficial Pistols 1st LP. Excellent quality studio demos.
European bootleg.

A&M demos excellent.
European bootleg.

Chris Spedding demos Majestic Studios, London 1976.
Australian bootleg

### Spunk (BLA 169)
**Side One** - Seventeen/ I'm in love/No feelings/ I wanna be me/Submission/ Anarchy in the UK
**Side Two** -
God save the Queen/ Problems/Pretty Vacant/ Liar/ Emi/ New York

### No Future UK (Spunk II)
GD 001/002
**Side One** - Pretty Vacant/ Seventeen/ Satellite/ No feelings/ I wanna be me/Submission/ Anarchy in the UK/
Anarchy in the UK (alternative take)
**Side Two** - No fun/ God Save the Queen/ Problems/ Pretty Vacant/ Liar/ Emi/
New York
Sleeve - Green and black cardboard wraparound

### Class of 76 (SEX 3531)
Punk compilation LP featuring Sex Pistols/Wire/
The Fall/ Buzzcocks/ Generation X/
Siouxsie & The Banshees

**Sex Pistols Tracks**
No feelings/ Pretty Vacant/ Problems
Sleeve - Full colour

# Sex Pistols Bootleg Bible:-

**Whitmans Punk Sampler**
Punk compilation featuring Damned/Ramones/Patti Smith/Iggy Pop/TomPetty/Talking Heads/Runaways/Sex Pistols
Sex Pistols one track `Anarchy in the UK' from TV `So it goes'
Sleeve - Coloured slick

Compilation Punk?? Tom Petty?? Must be American.

**St Albans Bash** (SEX 3523)
**Side One** - Stepping stone/ No feelings/no fun/ Substitute/ Problems/ Satellite/ No lip/ New York
**Side Two** - Carry on the Sex Pistols - interviews including Grundy, Thames TV special, Cock/Jones interview and Anarchy on `So it goes'.
Sleeve - Full colour

Side 1 claims to be St Albans, 2 August 1976 but is El Paradise, Soho 3 April 1976.
Australian bootleg.

**Nashville** (SEX 24)
**Side One** - Did you no wrong/ No lip/Lazy sod/NewYork/ Watcha gonna do about it / Stepping stone/ Submission/Satellite
**Side Two** - No feelings/ Pretty Vacant/No fun/ Substitute/ Problems/Understanding/ Did you no wrong
Sleeve - Full colour cartoon sleeve

Live Nashville Rooms, London 23 April 1976, plus last two tracks Aylesbury 2 February 1976.
Swedish bootleg.

# Sex Pistols Bootleg Bible:-

Live from Lesser Free Trade Hall, Manchester 4 June 1976.
European bootleg.

**The Good Time Music of the Sex Pistols (PFP)**
**Side One** - Did you no wrong/ Don't give me no lip child/ Seventeen/ Stepping stone/ New York/
Watcha gonna do about it
**Side Two** - Substitute/ Pretty Vacant/ Problems/ No fun
Sleeve - B/W

Live 100 Club 20 October 1976.
Japanese bootleg.

**100 Club - Punk Festival (SP 3068)**
**Side One** - No feelings/ Substitute/ Pretty Vacant/ Problems/ No fun/
Anarchy in the UK/
I wanna be me
**Side Two** - Seventeen/ New York/ No lip/ Stepping stone/ Satellite/ Sub-mission
Sleeve - Blue and white

Live at the 76 Club, Burton-on-Trent, England 24 October 1976.
European bootleg

**Indecent Exposure (5047)**
**Side One** - Anarchy in the UK/ I wanna be me/ I'm a lazy sod/ New York/
Don't give me no lip child/ Stepping stone/ Submission
**Side Two** - Liar/ Substitute/ No feelings/ no fun/ Pretty Vacant/ Problems
Sleeve - B/W with red newspaper cutting style wraparound; comes with rude insert and in plastic sleeve

# Sex Pistols Bootleg Bible:-

**Anarchy in Sweden**
(GUN 001)
**Side One** - Anarchy in the UK/ I wanna be me/ Seventeen/ Holidays in the Sun
**Side Two** - Emi/ No feelings/ Pretty Vacant/ Problems/ God save the Queen
Sleeve - `Sex Pistols' stamped red ink on cover; safety pin through sleeve - 300 only

Live Discotheque Beach, Halmstad, Sweden 15 July 1977.
European bootleg.

**Bad Boys in Sweden**
(SEX 3521)
**Side One** - Anarchy in the UK/ I wanna be me/ Seventeen/ New York/ Emi/ Submission/ Problems/God save the Queen/ Pretty Vacant
**Side Two** - Anarchy in the UK/ I wanna be me/ Seventeen/ New York/ Emi/No feelings/ Pretty Vacant/ Problems/ God save the Queen
Sleeve - Full colour

Side One Live Beach Disco, Halmstad 5 July 1977
Side Two Live Karen Stockholm 21 July 1977
Australian bootleg.

**Bad Boys** (PECCA BB 77)
**Side One** - Anarchy in the UK/ I wanna be me/I'm a lazy sod/ New York/ Emi
**Side Two** - Sub-mission/ Problems/ God save the Queen/ Pretty Vacant
Sleeve - Colour mock of Sgt. Pepper's sleeve

Live Happy House Stockholm, Sweden 23 July 1977
Swedish bootleg.

# Sex Pistols Bootleg Bible:-

**Tour of Scandinavia** (SP 3117)
**Side One** - Anarchy in the UK/ I wanna be me/ Seventeen/ New York/ Emi/ No feelings
**Side Two** - Pretty Vacant/ Problems/ God save the Queen/ I wanna be me/ Did you no wrong/ No fun/ Satellite
Sleeve - Blue and white

Live Beach Party Halmstad, Sweden 15 July 1977 - last four tracks are the B-side versions of Pistols 4 singles.
Japanese bootleg.

**Sweden** (UD 6557)
**Side One** - Anarchy in the UK/ I wanna be me/ Seventeen/ New York/ Emi
**Side Two** - Submission/ Problems/ God save the Queen/ Pretty Vacant
Side Three - Anarchy in the UK/ I wanna be me/ Seventeen/ New York/ Emi
Side Four - No feelings/ Pretty Vacant/ Problems/ God save the Queen
Sleeve - Blue and white

Sides 1 & 2 - Beach Disco Halmstad 15 July 1977
Sides 3 & 4 - Karen, Sweden 27 July 1977
Japanese Double LP bootleg.

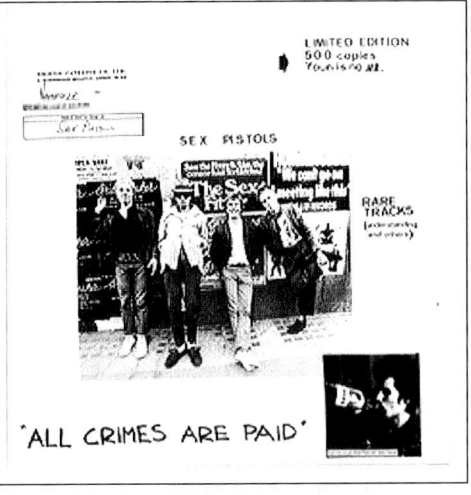

**All Crimes are Paid**
Viril (SBP-301)
**Side One** - Watcha gonna do about it (Studio 76)/Substitute; Did you no wrong (Burton, 9/1976)/ Satellite (Studio 76)/ Emi (Stockholm 28/7/77)/ No feelings (Burton 9/76)
**Side Two** - Watcha gonna do about it (Nashville, London 24/4/76)/ Belsen was a gas (San Fran 14/1/78)/ Belsen was a gas (Sid & Heartbreakers Max's, Kansas City 30/9/78)/ Belson was a gas (P.I.L. Rainbow Theatre 26/12/78)/New York; Understanding (Burton 9/76)
Sleeve - B/W wraparound

Compilation 500 numbered only ...
European bootleg.

# Sex Pistols Bootleg Bible:-

**Sex Pistols File**
**Sides 1 & 2** - Re-release `Spunk' (BLA 169)
**Sides 3 & 4** - Re-release `Indecent Exposure' (SP 6148)
**Sides 5 & 6** - Re-release `Welcome to the Rodeo' (SP 2800)
**Sides 7 & 8** - Re-release `Gun Control' (SP 2900)
Sleeve - Black box with printed B/W wraparound

250 numbered copies. See the above titles in this chapter for track listings.
American bootleg.

**`Rot-n-Roll'** (K&S 023)
**Side One -**
God save the Queen/ I wanna be me/ Seventeen/ New York/ Bodies/ Sub-mission
**Side Two** - Holidays in the Sun/ Emi/ No feelings/ Problems/ Pretty Vacant/ Anarchy in the USA
Sleeve - Slick (insert)

Live in Atlanta 5 January 1978 - Pistols' 1st US show. This album pressed on multi-coloured vinyl.
American bootleg.

**My Name is John**
(AMNESIA LG 001)
Sleeve - B/W picture of Pistols' on stage at this gig

Live in Atlanta 5 January 1978
Same gig as above but excellent quality mixing desk.
American bootleg.

# Sex Pistols Bootleg Bible:-

Live in San Antonio, Texas 8 January 1978.
Australian bootleg.

**Anarchy in the USA**
(SEX 3522)
**Side One** - Anarchy in the UK/
God save the Queen/
I wanna be me/ Seventeen/
New York/ Bodies
**Side Two** - Sub-mission/
Holidays in the sun/ Emi/
No feelings/ Problems/
Pretty Vacant
Sleeve - Full colour

Live Dallas, Texas Longhorn Ballroom 10 January 1978.
American bootleg.

Welcome to the Rodeo
(SP 2800)
**Side One -**
God save the Queen/
I wanna be me/ Seventeen/
New York/ Emi/ Bodies
**Side Two -** No feelings/
Problems/ Pretty Vacant/
Anarchy in the UK/ No fun
Sleeve - B/W printed, slick stuck-on cover

Live at Winterland Ballroom, Winterland 14 January 1978
American bootleg.
**Sex Pistols' last ever gig ... R.I.P.**

**Gun Control** (SP 2900)
**Side One -**
God save the Queen/
I wanna be me/ Seventeen/
New York/Emi/
Belsen was a gas/ Bodies/
Holidays in the sun
**Side Two** - Liar/ No feelings/
Problems/ Pretty Vacant/
Anarchy in the USA/ No fun
Sleeve - B/W slick stuck-on
white sleeve

# Sid Vicious Alive and Well

**The Sid Vicious Experience Jack Boots and Dirty Looks**

**Side One** - C'mon everybody/ Stepping stone/ No lip/ I wanna be your dog
**Side Two** - Belsen was a gas/ Chatterbox/ Tight pants/ My way
Sleeve - B/W

Sid's last lament - a gig to send Sid off to America.
His group was Steve New (guitar), Glen Matlock (bass), Rat Scabies (drums), Nancy Spungen (backing vocals), Sid (vocals). Electric Ballroom, London 15 August 1978. European bootleg

**Sid Vicious - Live** (JSR 21)

**Side One** - Search and destroy/ I wanna be your dog/ Something else/ Belsen was a gas
**Side Two** - Steppin' stone/ Chinese rocks/ My way/ 10-min ago (Take a chance on me)
Sleeve - Red lettering on B/W background wraparound

Sid plays Max's Kansas City (New York club); Group - Mick Jones (Clash/guitar), Killer Kane (NY Dolls, bass), Jerry Nolan (NY Dolls, drums)  Max's Kansas City NY 7 September 1978. American bootleg.

**Vicious Burger** (VD 6336)
Sleeve - Deluxe red and black

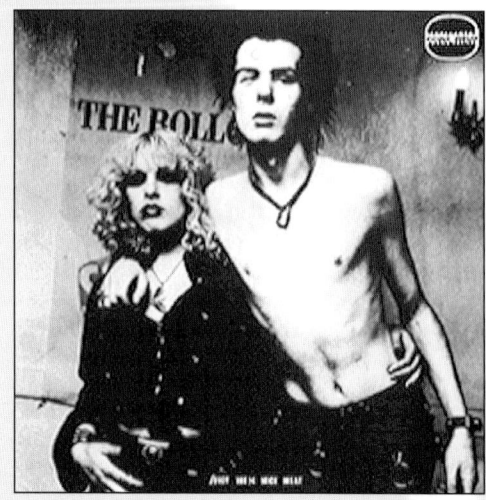

Same gig as above, Max's Kansas City 7 September 1978.
Better sleeve/better quality.
Japanese bootleg.

Sid R.I.P.

# Sex Pistols Live Gig Guide...Confirmed Sightings

## 1975

| | |
|---|---|
| 6/11/75 | St Martin's School of Art, London WC2 |
| 7/11/75 | Central School of Art, Holborn |
| 21/11/75 | Westfield College, Finchley Road, NW3 |
| 28/11/75 | Queen Elizabeth College, Kensington W8 |
| 5/12/75 | Chelsea School of Art, Manresa Road, SW3 |
| 9/12/75 | Ravensbourne College of Art, Chistlehurst |

## 1976

| | |
|---|---|
| 12/2/76 | Marquee Club, London |
| 14/2/76 | Andrew Logan's Party, Butlers Wharf, Tower Bridge |
| 19/2/76 | Hertfordshire College of Art, St Albans |
| 20/2/76 | College of Higher Education, High Wycombe |
| 21/2/76 | Welwyn Garden City |
| 25/3/76 | Hertfordshire College of Art, St Albans |
| 30/3/76 | 100 Club, Oxford Street, W1 |
| 3/4/76 | The Nashville Rooms, Kensington, W8 |
| 4/4/76 | El Paradise Strip Club, Soho, London |
| 23/4/76 | Nashville Rooms, Kensington, London |
| 29/4/76 | Nashville Rooms, Kensington, London |
| 5/5/76 | The Babalu Disco, Finchley Road, London |
| 11/5/76 | 100 Club, Oxford Street, W1 |
| 19/5/76 | Northallerton, Yorkshire |
| 20/5/76 | Penthouse, Scarborough |
| 21/5/76 | Town Hall, Middlesborough |
| 25/5/76 | 100 Club, Oxford Street, W1 |
| 30/5/76 | Reading University, London |
| 4/6/76 | Lesser Free Trade Hall, Manchester |
| 15/6/76 | 100 Club, Oxford Street, W1 |
| 17/6/76 | Walthamstow Assembly Hall, Walthamstow, London |
| 29/6/76 | 100 Club, Oxford Street, W1 |
| 3/7/76 | Pier Pavillion, Hastings |
| 4/7/76 | Black Swan, Sheffield |
| 6/7/76 | 100 Club, Oxford Street, W1 |
| 9/7/76 | Lyceum Ballroom, London |
| 10/7/76 | The Sundown, Charing Cross Road, London |
| 20/7/76 | Lesser Free Trade Hall, Manchester |
| 10/8/76 | 100 Club, Oxford Street, W1 |
| 14/8/76 | Barbarella's, Birmingham |
| 21/8/76 | Boat Club, Nottingham |
| 29/8/76 | Screen on the Green, Islington, London |
| 31/8/76 | 100 Club, Oxford Street, W1 |
| 2/9/76 | Nags Head, High Wycombe |

# Sex Pistols Live Gig Guide...Confirmed Sightings 1976

|  |  | |
|---|---|---|
| 3/9/76 | Club de Chalet du Lac, Paris, France | **first foreign show Paris** |
| 4/9/76 | Club de Chalet du Lac, Paris, France | |
| 12/9/76 | Fordgreen Ballroom, Leeds | |
| 13/9/76 | Quaintways, Chester | |
| 15/9/76 | Lodestar, Blackburn | |
| 17/9/76 | Chelmsford Prison, Chelmsford | |
| 20/9/76 | 100 Club, Oxford Street, W1 | **100 Club Punk Festival** |
| 21/9/76 | Top Rank, Cardiff | |
| 22/9/76 | Swansea | |
| 24/9/76 | 76 Club, Burton upon Trent | |
| 27/9/76 | Outlook Club, Doncaster | |
| 28/9/76 | Guildford | |
| 29/9/76 | Strikes Club, Stoke | |
| 30/9/76 | Cleopatra's, Derby | |
| 1/10/76 | Didsbury College, Manchester | |
| 12/10/76 | Technical College, Dundee | **Sex Pistols Holland (1)** |
| 13/10/76 | Lafayette Club, Wolverhampton | |
| 14/10/76 | Birkenhead | |
| 15/10/76 | Eric's, Liverpool | |
| 20/10/76 | Bogarts, Birmingham | |
| 21/10/76 | Queensway Hall, Dunstable | |
| 15/11/76 | Notre Dame Hall, Leicester Place, London | |
| 19/11/76 | Polytechnic, Hendon, London | |
| 29/11/76 | Lancaster Polytechnic, Coventry | |
| 6/12/76 | Polytechnic, Leeds | **the only 3 gigs from the 'anarchy in the UK' tour to be played** |
| 9/12/76 | Electric Circus, Manchester | |
| 14/12/76 | Castle Cinema, Caerphilly | |
| 19/12/76 | Electric Circus, Manchester | |
| 20/12/76 | Winter Gardens, Cleethorpes | |
| 21/12/76 | Woods Centre, Plymouth | |
| 22/12/76 | Woods Centre, Plymouth | |

# Sex Pistols Live Gig Guide

# 1977

| Date | Venue | Tour |
|---|---|---|
| 5/1/77 | Paradiso Club, Amsterdam | **Sex Pistols Holland (1)** |
| 6/1/77 | Art Centre, Rotterdam | |
| 7/1/77 | Paradise Club, Amsterdam | |
| 21/3/77 | Notre Dame Hall, Leicester Place, London | |
| 3/4/77 | Screen on the Green, Islington, London | |
| 16/6/77 | Famous Riverboat Cruise, River Thames, London | **Jubilee boat trip** |
| 13/7/77 | Daddy's Dance Hall, Copenhagen, Denmark | **Sex Pistols Scandinavian tour** |
| 14/7/77 | Daddy's Dance Hall, Copenhagen, Denmark | |
| 15/7/77 | Beach Party, Halmstad, Sweden | |
| 16/7/77 | Mogambo Disco, Helsing Borg, Sweden | |
| 17/7/77 | Disco 42, Jonkoping, Sweden | |
| 19/7/77 | Club Zebra, Kristine Hamn, Sweden | |
| 20/7/77 | Pinguinen Restaurant, Oslo, Norway | |
| 21/7/77 | Student Ssamfundet Club, Trondheim, Sweden | |
| 23/7/77 | Barbarella's, Vaxjo, Sweden | |
| 24/7/77 | Barbarella's, Vaxjo, Sweden | |
| 27/7/77 | Happy House, Stockholm, Sweden | |
| 28/7/77 | Happy House, Stockholm, Sweden | |

under the name of
- SPOTS
- Tax Exiles
- Special Guest
- Acne Rabble
- Hamsters
- A Mystery Band of International Repute

| Date | Venue | Tour |
|---|---|---|
| 19/8/77 | Lafayette Club, Wolverhampton | **SPOTS tour Sex Pistols tour secretly** |
| 24/8/77 | Outlook Club, Doncaster | |
| 25/8/77 | Scarborough | |
| 26/8/77 | Rock Garden, Middlesborough | |
| 31/8/77 | Woods Centre, Plymouth | |
| 1/9/77 | Winter Gardens, Penzance | |
| 5/12/77 | Eksit Club, Rotterdam, Holland | **Sex Pistols Holland (2)** |
| 6/12/77 | Maastricht, Holland | |
| 7/12/77 | Pozjet Club, Tilburg, Holland | |
| 8/12/77 | Arnhem, Holland | |
| 9/12/77 | Eindhoven, Holland | |
| 10/12/77 | Groningen, Holland | |
| 11/12/77 | MAF Centrum, Maasbree, Holland | |
| 13/12/77 | Wimschoten, Holland | |
| 14/12/77 | Eksit Club, Rotterdam, Holland | |
| 16/12/77 | Brunel University, Uxbridge | **Nevermind the bans tour** |
| 17/12/77 | Mr George's, Coventry | |
| 19/12/77 | Nikkees Club, Keighley | |
| 21/12/77 | Lafayettes Club, Wolverhampton | |
| 23/12/77 | Stowaway Club, Newport | |
| 24/12/77 | Links Pavillion, Cromer | |
| 25/12/77 | Ivanhoe's Club, Huddersfield | |

# Sex Pistols Live Gig Guide

## 1978

| | |
|---|---|
| 5/1/78 | Great South East Music Hall, Atlanta, USA |
| 6/1/78 | Taliesyn Ballroom, Memphis, USA |
| 8/1/78 | Randy's Rodeo, San Antonio, Texas, USA |
| 9/1/78 | Kingfisher Club, Baton Rouge, USA |
| 10/1/78 | Longhall Ballroom, Dallas, USA |
| 12/1/78 | Cains Ballroom, Tulsa, USA |
| 14/1/78 | Winterland Ballroom, Winterland, USA |

**Anarchy in the USA**

## R.I.P.

## "ever get the feeling you've been cheated"

J. Rotten

**WINTERLAND BALLROOM**
**WINTERLAND USA**
**14 JANUARY 1978**

# "Never Mind the Sex Pistols ... Here's the Filthy Lucre"

The Sex Pistols first took us by storm in the Superficial Seventies, left us to our Excessive Eighties and have returned via the Nostalgic Nineties, ending years of rumours, lies and all kinds of speculation. They're back.

All four original members - Johnny Rotten (vocals), Steve Jones (guitar), Paul Cook (drums) and Glen Matlock (bass) - appeared at a press conference in London on Monday, 18 March 1996 to announce a headlining world tour commencing 21 June and plans to release a newly recorded live album in late July on Virgin Records.

The press conference took place at the historic punk venue where the cultural insurrection began in 1976: The 100 Club. The words on the invitation to the event: **"NEVER MIND THE SEX PISTOLS ... HERE'S THE FILTHY LUCRE"**.

The upcoming live album will be recorded at one of the first few gigs on the tour, which will encompass dates in UK and Europe (including some festival performances as headlines) through July 20. The band will then head out on a six-week summer tour of the US (they only played eight American shows back in January 1978).

The PISTOLS will subsequently launch first-ever tours of Australia and New Zealand (October) and Japan (November) including several shows at Budokan.

Confirmed 1996 tour dates are as follows:

| Date | Country | Venue |
| --- | --- | --- |
| Friday 21 June | Finland | Messila Festival |
| Saturday 22 June | Germany | Munich Hall 55 |
| Sunday 23 June | UK | Finsbury Park, London |
| Wednesday 26 June | Sweden | Stockholm Naval Museum |
| Friday 28 June | Denmark | Roskilde Festival |
| Saturday 29 June | Germany | Hamburg Bahrenfield |
| Sunday 30 June | Switzerland | TBA |
| Tuesday 2 July | Spain | Madrid Palace |
| Thursday 4 July | France | Paris Zenith |
| Saturday 6 July | Germany | Berlin Arena |
| Sunday 7 July | Czech Rep | Prague Sportshall |
| Tuesday 9 July | Slovenia | Ljubljana Hala Tivoli |
| Wednesday 10 July | Italy | Rome Curva Stadio Olimpico |
| Thursday 11 July | Italy | Milan Parco Aquatica |
| Saturday 13 July | Germany | Munster Ochtrup Festival |
| Tuesday 16 July | UK | Glasgow SECC |
| Wednesday 17 July | Northern Ireland | Belfast Maysfield Leisure Centre |
| Thursday 18 July | Eire | Dublin RDS |
| Saturday 20 July | Belgium | Zeebrugge Belga Beach Festival |

# "Never Mind the Sex Pistols ... Here's the Filthy Lucre"

**Press Fax** sent out to the media announcing press conference to be held at the 100 Club Oxford Street

**Press Pack** given to the Media on arrival of the press conference, containing interview from 1977, press cuttings, B/W Pictures and a copy of 'Never Trust a Hippie' Special edition booklet.

**Poster** Advertising the Sex Pistols gig at Finsbury Park. London 23rd June 1996.

**By the time you've read this you may well have seen the SEX PISTOLS play one of there reunion shows in your town**